"I love everything that Scott Sauls writes. Scott and Patti have also become friends to Nick and me, encouraging us in our work of preaching the gospel, confronting the darkness, and fighting for the hearts of those who are oppressed and vulnerable. In *Irresistible Faith*, Scott makes us want to love Jesus more, and in loving Jesus more, to do our part in leaving the world better than we found it. I'm certain that his words will have a similar effect on you."

—CHRISTINE CAINE, FOUNDER OF A21 AND PROPEL WOMEN

"The Christian Community in all its terrific diversity has provided great hope to the world for two millennia. Sometimes I wonder whether the Christian community is still curious about objective truth, especially when that truth might cost their tribe its power objective. If Christians continue down this road, I think the Christian community will dwindle. I don't want that to happen and so I'm grateful for this book and for Scott Sauls. I miss the kind of church Scott is describing in this book, and I don't think I am alone."

—DONALD MILLER, AUTHOR OF *BLUE LIKE JAZZ* AND *BUILDING A STORYBRAND*

"Scott Sauls has a way of reminding us what we're here for. *Irresistible Faith* is an important call to resist the urge to lobby and position ourselves, but rather to be driven by gospel-powered love. As both an author and our family's pastor, Scott consistently challenges us to be 'people of the Book,' and for that I am grateful."

—RAECHEL MYERS, FOUNDER AND CEO OF SHE READS TRUTH

"How we long for our faith, our lives, and our walk with Jesus to be irresistible. But it's easy for us to get tripped up in our comfortable, self-absorbed American way of life. Sadly, our non-believing friends notice. They call us hypocrites and judgmental. Many times they get it right and instead of being attracted, are repelled. Thank God for Scott Sauls and his vision to remind us of *Irresistible Faith*. This book is an antidote to much that is wrong with our Western version of Christianity. We hope it will be for you, as it is for us, a guidebook to find our way through—and back—to all that Jesus intended our lives to reflect."

—GABE AND REBEKAH LYONS, AUTHORS AND FOUNDERS OF Q

"Over the past ten years I have had way more questions about my faith than answers, and Scott Sauls has stood in the midst of those questions with thoughtfulness and prayerful examination. *Irresistible Faith* is like having our friend Scott with us through the wondering, exploring what it can look like when we shed robotic routine and give our faith a chance to become magnetically real to one another."

—ELISABETH HASSELBECK, AUTHOR OF *POINT OF VIEW*

"Scott Sauls, a minister who became an 'accidental author,' is marvelous at both callings. *Irresistible Faith* shows why. It is a compelling, honest, transparent, and deeply hopeful book. Scott's perspective helps us see ancient truths in fresh ways. Written in a way that is accessible and thoughtful, balanced and winsome, Scott allows the Christian faith to speak for itself, to come alive, to make it relevant to the here and now. In an age when too many Christians are discrediting their faith, Scott is modeling what it should be. That is a gift to the rest of us."

—PETER WEHNER, SENIOR FELLOW OF THE ETHICS AND PUBLIC POLICY CENTER, *NEW YORK TIMES* OP-ED WRITER, COAUTHOR OF *CITY OF A MAN*, AND SENIOR WHITE HOUSE ADVISOR TO FORMER PRESIDENT GEORGE W. BUSH

"Scott Sauls shows us how to balance conviction with civility by reminding us that we can only love our neighbors as ourselves when we have first learned to see others—and ourselves—as image bearers."

—JOHN INAZU, AUTHOR OF *CONFIDENT PLURALISM*

"As we read *Irresistible Faith*, we couldn't stop nodding our heads with a resounding 'Yes!' Scott Sauls beautifully exposes the kind of Christians our world is desperate to see, and certainly compels each of us to live as we were created: Holy-Spirit-animated, God-oriented, people-loving, scripture-believing, community-building, Jesus-loving people. Yes to that!"

—AARON AND JAMIE IVEY, PASTOR OF WORSHIP + CREATIVITY
AT THE AUSTIN STONE AND AUTHOR OF *STEAL AWAY HOME*,
HOST OF *THE HAPPY HOUR WITH JAMIE IVEY PODCAST*
AND BESTSELLING AUTHOR OF *IF YOU ONLY KNEW*

"With biblical clarity, personal transparency, and a relentlessly winsome spirit, Scott Sauls shows us how authentic Christianity is attractive Christianity. *Irresistible Faith* is a timely and reliable road map for those seeking to restore the damaged witness and public reputation of Christians. It offers a refreshing reminder of this oft-neglected truth: personal transformation in the gospel and commitment to Christian community are essential, rather than optional, to the fruitful pursuit of Christ's mission. If you want to learn how the grace of God makes us the 'light of the world' in all of life, read this book!"

—DUKE KWON, LEAD PASTOR OF GRACE
MERIDIAN HILL, WASHINGTON, DC

"Scott Sauls has written a compelling book that does something remarkable in both your head and your heart. He accurately diagnoses the angst and tension many of us feel around our current version of Christianity, and then paints a picture and pathway to a personally inspiring, culturally credible faith. I found myself resonating on a deep level with his insight, humor, depth, and I honestly and personally know that he writes out of a life that models these teachings so well. I believe this book will go a long way in helping the church become more like the one Jesus had in mind."

—JON TYSON, LEAD PASTOR OF CHURCH OF THE CITY, NYC, AND AUTHOR OF *THE BURDEN IS LIGHT*

"The challenge with Christianity isn't that non-Christians don't know any Christians. The challenge is that they do. And when they see us, they see a very resistible version of Christianity. That's one of the many reasons I'm so thankful for Scott Sauls's voice. *Irresistible Faith* is a wake-up call to all people who follow Jesus to live our lives with a much deeper integrity that makes our faith irresistible."

—CAREY NIEUWHOF, FOUNDING PASTOR OF CONNEXUS CHURCH AND AUTHOR OF *DIDN'T SEE IT COMING*

"Scott Sauls uses a straight talking, culturally relevant style to disarm common characterizations of Christians by pointing us back to Christ in our workplaces, neighborhoods, and communities. He paints a picture of true Christianity, the kind that is so lifegiving that even our critics would be sad if we disappeared. Read *Irresistible Faith* alone or with a group, and embrace a fresh vision to abide in Christ all day, every day—at work, at school, in conflict, and more—not just for an hour on Sundays. Because now more than ever, the world needs Christians with an irresistible faith."

—MISSY WALLACE, EXECUTIVE DIRECTOR OF THE NASHVILLE INSTITUTE FOR FAITH AND WORK

"Scott Sauls speaks through these pages in the same compelling way that he connects with me and the rest of our church congregation in Nashville every Sunday—with a vulnerable authenticity that points to the Giver of grace and God's promises through Scripture at every turn. This book is a much-needed reminder that perfection is not a prerequisite for irresistible faith. All are welcome to take part in reaching a lost and hurting world, including a 'busted-up sinner' like me. God is going to use Scott's words in a powerful way."

—MATTHEW WEST, SINGER-SONGWRITER AND NINE-TIME DOVE AWARD NOMINEE

"It can be so easy for the world to look at Christians and believe our faith is self-serving and insular, but this book is a timely reminder that the good news of Jesus Christ that transforms his followers is also supposed to transform the world. Encouraging us to believe that the best of our faith is lived out when we pour out to others the very love we ourselves receive from a gracious God, *Irresistible Faith* provides us with the tools we so desperately need to lay down our selfish inclinations and be sold out to God and his mission. I'm so grateful that Scott Sauls continues to challenge and equip us to live larger than ourselves in this book and in his ministry."

—JENNY YANG, VICE PRESIDENT FOR ADVOCACY AND POLICY AT WORLD RELIEF

IRRESISTIBLE FAITH

ALSO BY SCOTT SAULS

Jesus Outside the Lines

Befriend

From Weakness to Strength

IRRESISTIBLE FAITH

FAITH

BECOMING THE KIND OF CHRISTIAN
THE WORLD CAN'T RESIST

SCOTT SAULS

NELSON
BOOKS

An Imprint of Thomas Nelson

Published in Nashville, Tennessee, by Nelson Books, an imprint of Thomas Nelson. Nelson Books and Thomas Nelson are registered trademarks of HarperCollins Christian Publishing, Inc.

Published in association with the literary association of Wolgemuth & Associates, Inc.

Thomas Nelson titles may be purchased in bulk for educational, business, fund-raising, or sales promotional use. For information, please e-mail SpecialMarkets@ThomasNelson.com.

Unless otherwise noted, Scripture quotations are taken from the ESV® Bible (The Holy Bible, English Standard Version®). Copyright © 2001 by Crossway, a publishing ministry of Good News Publishers. Used by permission. All rights reserved.

Scripture quotations marked THE MESSAGE are from *The Message*. Copyright © by Eugene H. Peterson 1993, 1994, 1995, 1996, 2000, 2001, 2002. Used by permission of NavPress. All rights reserved. Represented by Tyndale House Publishers, Inc.

Any internet addresses, phone numbers, or company or product information printed in this book are offered as a resource and are not intended in any way to be or to imply an endorsement by Thomas Nelson, nor does Thomas Nelson vouch for the existence, content, or services of these sites, phone numbers, companies, or products beyond the life of this book.

ISBN 978-1-4002-0179-2 (TP)
ISBN 978-1-4002-0180-8 (eBook)

Library of Congress Cataloging-in-Publication Data
Names: Sauls, Scott, author.
Title: Irresistible faith : becoming the kind of Christian the world can't resist / Scott Sauls.
Description: Nashville : Thomas Nelson, 2019. | Includes bibliographical references.
Identifiers: LCCN 2018028668 | ISBN 9781400201792 (pbk.)
Subjects: LCSH: Christian life.
Classification: LCC BV4501.3 .S2829 2019 | DDC 248.4--dc23 LC record available at https://lccn.loc.gov/2018028668

Printed in the United States of America

19 20 21 22 23   LSC   10 9 8 7 6 5 4 3 2 1

To Matt:
My brother by blood,
and my brother in Christ.

CONTENTS

FOREWORD BY
BOB GOFF

WHEN I WAS IN COLLEGE, I took a few months and hitch-hiked around New England. I met some really interesting people along the way, and a few creepy ones too. In truth, I suppose I was looking a little creepy myself as a barefoot nineteen-year-old with flaming red hair down to my shoulders, torn jeans, and a stained T-shirt. I didn't need much, just a ride and a pair of shoes.

When people pulled over to give me a ride, I tried to size them up before I got in the car, and they were no doubt trying figure out whether I was safe before they picked me up. I suppose the same thing happens in our faith communities every day. We want to know who we can trust and who we ought to pass by; who we ought to go with and who we should avoid. In short, we're all try-ing to figure out how to live out our faith and who to do it with. Scott is a good friend of mine and is a person I trust. This book has helped me engage with some of those questions I still have about my faith. I think it will help you with yours.

I had been stuck with my thumb out on a highway outside Bangor, Maine, for a long time. A car pulled over with a kind, bearded man at the wheel. I climbed in the passenger seat and the driver introduced himself to me in a humble voice. "My name is Don," he said, sticking out his hand a little tentatively. Don apparently didn't have a last name, and I was okay with that. He was kind of like Jesus or MacGyver or Cher, I figured.

It turned out Don was a hermit and lived alone in the woods. I had heard about hermits, but I don't think I had met one before and I wondered how they lived their lives. Other than the few things I was pretty sure were true, like the fact that they lived alone, I didn't have a lot of reference points. Some of us feel this way about our own faith. We want to follow Jesus. We may have met a few people who said they did. But we just don't know how to do it. Yet while there's no rule book for how to live like a hermit, fortunately, Jesus left behind a lot of information about how we could live like one of his followers. You'll find a great deal of that information in this book.

Some Christians live like hermits in their faith. There are a few things that may have led them into isolation. Perhaps at some point they started caring more about what their faith looked like than what it was. Maybe their opinions about people they disagreed with started blocking their view of these same people as being made by God in his image. Possibly along the way they got burned by people who also said they were following Jesus but acted like they didn't. If this is you, this book isn't just an invitation to come home; it's as if Jesus were pulling over and asking if you want to go there with him.

It was getting late, we were still driving, and Don invited me to stay at his house that night. In a moment of brilliant foolishness, I agreed. The house Don lived in was far from everyone. It had no electricity and no plumbing, just a tank of propane and a small oven. He drew his water from a well behind the house and bartered with his neighbors for everything he needed in his life. Despite that, it would be a hermit whom God would use to teach me the importance of living in community with him.

I didn't spend just a night with Don; I spent a month with him.

Each morning Don and I made candlesticks and dropped them off at different people's houses. The afternoons were spent in these same people's gardens, picking vegetables for dinner. From an unusually large patch of rhubarb, we picked the stalks, took them home, and made rhubarb pies we would drop off the next morning as we bartered for what we needed. In short, we used what we knew how to do to get whatever else we needed.

I think most of us want our faith to be more real. The problem is, we don't use what we've already got to get what we need. We think we can trade good conduct for God's grace, but we can't; and when we try to, we look like orphans. We all want our faith to look like it's working, too, but we overlook the beauty that can be found only within the authenticity of letting the people around us know when we're lost and hurting. Instead of admitting to the pain and isolation we've experienced in our lives, we distract ourselves with things that won't last and, in the process, forget our absolute need for a savior. The reminder Scott gives us in this book is that God has not left us alone: he's given us each other, he's given us communities of faith to go deeper with, and he's given us his Son. In other words, we don't need to live like hermits anymore.

This book is an invitation for us to return to the most authentic version of our faith. It's also an invitation to join, or create, an authentic community of people trying to go somewhere beautiful with their faith.

It was fall in Maine, and the leaves were just beginning to turn colors. All I thought I needed the day I met Don was a ride and a pair of shoes. What God knew I needed much more was a few reminders about how I could go deeper in my faith. Both Don and

I needed to risk a little to make those lessons happen. If you want to go deeper in your faith, you'll need to risk a little too.

Eventually, it was time to leave, and Don gave me a ride to the highway so I could start hitchhiking south. We said our goodbyes, and as I got out of the car Don reached into the back seat and handed me a bag. Inside was a pair of his shoes. I've still got them.

If we're willing to show up and risk a little, God will provide us what we need and someone to go with. What Scott has done in these pages is give us some beautiful reminders about what each of us needs and about the someone we can trust to go with. It isn't just a pair of shoes he's given us; it's Jesus.

—Bob Goff, author of *Love Does* and *Everybody, Always*

INTRODUCTION

THESE DAYS, THE WORD *CHRISTIAN* seems to evoke as many negative reactions as it does positive ones.

This bothers me.

Does it bother you?

Critics might summarize their feelings about Christians with these words attributed to Mahatma Gandhi: "I like your Christ, but I do not like your Christians. Your Christians are so unlike your Christ."[1]

More recently, San Francisco journalist Herb Caen said, "The trouble with born-again Christians is that they are an even bigger pain the second time around."[2]

And painfully—especially coming from an adult Christian convert who then became disenchanted with her church—Vampire Chronicles author Anne Rice wrote, "For those who care, and I understand if you don't: Today I quit being a Christian. I'm out. I remain committed to Christ as always but not to being 'Christian' or to being part of Christianity. It's simply impossible for me to 'belong' to this quarrelsome, hostile, disputatious, and deservedly infamous group. For ten years, I've tried. I've failed. I'm an outsider. My conscience will allow nothing else."[3]

Deservedly infamous. Ouch!

As a forgiven, loved, and Spirit-filled people, we can do better than this.

Can't we?

Christians certainly did at one time. Look no further than Luke's observation about first-century Christians in the book of Acts. Their quality of life was so rich, their worship so genuine, their life together so deep, and their neighbor-love so palpable, that they were "having favor with *all* the people" and "the Lord added to their number day by day those who were being saved" (Acts 2:47, emphasis added). So what went wrong? How did we end up alienating the world around us *from* Christ, rather than attracting it *to* Christ?

As the sentiments noted above make crystal clear, the people of Jesus often have not represented him well, and our poor representation has created a public relations nightmare for the movement that he began through his death, burial, and resurrection. In the eyes of a watching world, our lives are often perceived as being more lackluster than compelling, more contentious than kind, more self-centered than servant-like, more fickle than faithful, more materialistic than generous, more proud than humble.

Rather than shining as a light *to* the culture, we often become products *of* the culture. As those whom Christ has called the light of the world, the salt of the earth, and a city on a hill, we still have a long way to go.

Our generation of Christians is not the first to limp along in its calling to live as salt and light. Since Bible times and throughout history, we have fumbled again and again. Noah's drunkenness, Abraham's misogyny, Jacob's lies, Jesse's parental neglect, Elijah's self-pity, David's adultery and murder, Solomon's womanizing, Peter's abrasiveness and cowardice, and the Corinthian church's worldliness are only a few of the many biblical examples of stumbling saints.

Past and present history also reminds us of horrid things done in the name of Christ that would make the actual Christ want to turn over a table or two—Servetus burned at the stake, the Crusades, the Inquisition, the genocide of Native Americans, institutional slavery, white supremacy, signs reading "Fags Burn in Hell" raised at funerals, blind assertions that the 9/11 terrorist attacks were God's judgment on America . . . and more.

In his masterful exposition of Jesus' Sermon on the Mount, Dr. Martyn Lloyd-Jones said that Christians become a light *to* the world to the degree that they stand out as different *from* the world. The world does not thirst for a religious imitation of itself, nor does it thirst for an "us against them" moral turf war with its zealous religious neighbors. The world thirsts for a different kind of neighbor—not the kind who deny their fellow man, take up their comforts, and follow their dreams—but the kind who deny themselves, take up their crosses, and follow Jesus in his mission of loving a weary world to life. The world also thirsts for a new vision for being human, for pursuing and entering friendship, and for leaving things better than we found them. As Lloyd-Jones wrote, "The glory of the gospel is that when the Church is absolutely *different from the world*, she invariably attracts it."[4]

The problem isn't with Christianity as much as it is with our flawed approach to and understanding of Christianity. We have let ourselves become imbalanced, lopsided, and unfocused (much like the rigid, holier-than-thou Pharisees *and* the materialistic, secular Sadducees of the New Testament). To regain our footing, we need to begin following the whole Jesus and the whole Scripture, into the whole world, the whole time.

As one who longs to see Christianity return to a place of life-giving, contagious presence in the world, I am both haunted and motivated by the characterization in Acts of the early church. That description compels me to ask: What would it look like for

Christians to be reignited in this kind of faith for *our* time? What would it look like for us to become those who live most beautifully, love most deeply, and serve most faithfully in the places where we live, work, and play? What would it look like, as Tim Keller has said, for us to live so compellingly and lovingly in our neighborhoods, cities, and nations that if we were suddenly removed from the world, our nonbelieving neighbors would miss us terribly? What would it look like for Christians to become the *first* place people go for comfort when a life-altering diagnosis comes, when anxiety and depression hit, when a child goes astray, when a spouse files for divorce, or when a breadwinner loses a job? What would it look like for a woman with a crisis pregnancy to see the local church, not the local clinic, as her trustworthy source for love, non-judgment, practical support, wise counsel, and much-needed encouragement? What would it look like for the local church to become the most diverse and welcoming—rather than the most homogeneous and inhospitable—community on earth? What would it look like for Christians to become not only the best kind of friends, but the best kind of enemies, returning insults with kindness and persecution with prayers? What would it look like for Christians, en masse, to start loving and following the whole Jesus and the whole Scripture, the whole time, into the whole world?

In short, what would it look like for Gandhi sympathizers to say, "Your Christians are so *like* your Christ"; for Herb Caen to say that being born again makes people *better*, not worse; and for Anne Rice to want to follow Christ in the church, *alongside* other Christians?

What would it look like for Christians to become an *irresistible force* again, even among their nonbelieving friends, colleagues, and neighbors?

Scripture declares that Christians are sent out to emanate

Christ's aroma to the world (2 Cor. 2:15). They are carriers of his divine imprint, swept up by grace into the honored task of bringing down foretastes of heaven. Jesus declared that we would leave the world, as far as it depended on us, better than we found it. He declared that we would be a sign and shadow of a better world, a world that all have imagined but none have yet fully seen. He declared that over time our movement—rather, *his* movement through us—would become irresistible to people from every nation, tribe, and tongue.

The novelist and poet Madeleine L'Engle wrote that "we draw people to Christ not by loudly discrediting what they believe, by telling them how wrong they are and how right we are, but by showing them a light that is so lovely that they want with all their hearts to know the source of it."[5]

In spite of this checkered past and present shared by Christ-followers, I write this book as an optimist. I am optimistic because Jesus *still* intends to renew and love the world through his people. I am optimistic because the negative stories, as concerning as they are, don't tell the full story and, therefore, shouldn't be allowed to completely own the narrative. The negative stories aren't the whole story because for every poor representation of Christ, there are a thousand infectiously beautiful ones. For history is also illuminated by L'Engle's "light so lovely" and by a Christian way of life that is truly remarkable and beautiful.

History is peppered with these kinds of lives. For example, Christians have shown groundbreaking leadership in science (Pascal, Copernicus, Newton, Galileo, Lise Meitner, Francis Collins), healthcare (all those hospitals named after a saint), the arts and literature (Rembrandt, Bach, Dorothy Sayers, Dostoevsky, T. S. Eliot, Flannery O'Connor, Makoto Fujimura, Johnny Cash, Bono), the academy (all but one of the Ivy League universities were founded by Christians), and mercy and justice (William Wilberforce, Hannah More, Dorothy Day, George Mueller, Martin Luther King Jr.).

The identifying mark of the City of God is when citizens of the heavenly city become the very best citizens of the earthly one. To be on the side of Jesus is to be on the side of the world and its flourishing. The gospel of John tells us, "For God so loved the world, that he gave his only Son, that whoever believes in him should not perish but have eternal life" (John 3:16). This doesn't merely describe Christ and his mission; it also defines our purpose as his ambassadors to a lost and fractured world. To put it plainly, we are to love this world.

When Paul tells us to set our minds on things above instead of things on earth (Col. 3:2), we mustn't assume this means we should check out of the world. On the contrary, when we have our minds set on things above—that is, on things that center around God's concerns—we become checked in, not checked out, to the world that God so loved. Having been made new in Christ, we have also become his ambassadors in the world, "sent out" to be contagious contributors, not contemptible contrarians, to the world around us. We are meant to be neither holier-than-thou *enemies* of the culture on the one hand, nor lawless and avaricious *products* of the culture on the other. Instead, we are to become culture-*shapers* for the good and flourishing of all. We are meant to resist every urge to lobby and position ourselves to become a powerful and privileged "moral majority"; rather, we are to pursue our God-given and biblically mandated calling to be a fiercely love-driven, self-donating, prophetic minority.

I think it's time for us to embrace that vision once again, don't you?

It is heartening to see contemporary observers take note of how Christian belief, in its purest form, produces beautiful lives.

New York Times columnist Nicholas Kristof frequently writes of how today's Christians outnumber the rest of the world in volunteer hours and dollars given toward the alleviation of poverty and human suffering. The gay mayor of Portland, Oregon, Sam Adams, has spoken publicly about how positive his experience was partnering with local Christian churches to serve the vulnerable communities of Portland. Here in our Nashville community, an abortion provider who is beginning to engage with the claims and ways of Christ recently told a member of our church, "I want your God, whoever he or she is, to be my God"—which appears to be his way of saying, "I like your Christ, not in spite of your Christians, but because of them."

This is the kind of Christianity I want to be part of, and this is the kind of Christianity I am committed to pursue. It is a beautiful and, therefore, a *truer* Christianity that shines a light that is so lovely. It is a Christianity that mirrors the whole Christ and so offers a tired and sometimes cynical world a reason to pause and consider . . . and to start wishing it could be true.

As I hope this book will demonstrate, history has shown that when this kind of transformation occurs among Christians, the "irresistibility" factor soon emerges as a byproduct. Just as a healthy tree can't help but produce fruit, and as a lit candle can't help but produce light, well-formed followers of Christ can't help but become positive contributors to the places they live, work, and play. *Irresistible Faith* is an attempt to nudge us in that direction, away from worldliness and toward a world that thirsts for a hope that only Christ can provide.

Part I of the book is designed to help us draw closer to Christ, our ultimate source of nourishment and light. Part II explores how living in community with other believers is an essential component to this endeavor. And the final section encourages us to take the grace we have received from Christ and from each other into the world in a way that uplifts the poor, integrates faith and work, and leaves the world better than we found it.

Are you ready to embark on a journey with the irresistible Christ, alongside an irresistible community, to the end that we all, by the grace and power of Christ, become the kind of Christians the world can't resist?

If so, then Jesus says, "Come, follow me" (Matt. 19:21).

PART I

ABIDING IN THE IRRESISTIBLE CHRIST

*You follow your desires wherever they take you,
and you approve of yourself so long as you are not
obviously hurting anyone else. You figure that if the
people around you seem to like you, you must be good
enough. In the process you end up slowly turning
yourself into something a little less impressive than
you had originally hoped. A humiliating gap opens
up between your actual self and your desired self.*

— DAVID BROOKS

*"All that the Father gives me will come to me. . . . I
am the vine; you are the branches. Whoever abides
in me and I in him, he it is that bears much fruit, for
apart from me you can do nothing. If anyone does
not abide in me he is thrown away like a branch and
withers; and the branches are gathered, thrown
into the fire, and burned. If you abide in me, and*

*my words abide in you, ask whatever you wish,
and it will be done for you. By this my Father is
glorified, that you bear much fruit and so prove
to be my disciples. As the Father has loved me, so
have I loved you. Abide in my love. If you keep my
commandments, you will abide in my love, just as I
have kept my Father's commandments and abide in
his love. These things I have spoken to you, that my
joy may be in you, and that your joy may be full."*

—JESUS CHRIST

CHAPTER 1

BEING OKAY WITH
NOT BEING OKAY

FOR MOST HONEST CHRISTIANS, BECOMING like Jesus Christ—what Scripture calls *sanctification*—can be an anti-climactic process. No matter how much better we become over time, no matter how much more loving, joyful, peaceful, patient, kind, good, faithful, gentle, and self-controlled we are this year compared to last year (Gal. 5:22–23), we never progress in our character to the degree that we once hoped we would. Ironically, the more like Jesus we actually become, the less like Jesus we tend to feel.

When I first became a Christian, I had a brimming optimism about becoming a better version of myself. This, after all, is the promise of God to all who trust in Jesus—he will not merely help us turn over a new leaf; he will actually give us a new life. As a newly born child of God, I was a new creation. The old Scott was gone, and the new Scott had come (2 Cor. 5:17). The Holy Spirit had taken up residence in me, which meant that the same power that raised Jesus from the dead was living in me. This power would give me faith to trust and follow God's Word and God's ways over my own flawed feelings, impulses, and ideas. It would give me hope in the face of life's sorrows, letdowns, and uncertainties. Most of all, it would enhance my ability to love God and others. Through this newfound faith in Christ, I could become the kind of friend, neighbor, spouse, and contributor whose *irresistible faith* would be remembered and celebrated—even long after I'm gone.

Like many Christians in their newfound faith, I felt really good about the kind of person I was destined to become in Christ. I would, as the apostle Paul has written, be able to "do all things through [Christ] who strengthens me" (Phil. 4:13). It was only a matter of time before I would become the very best version of myself. Or so I thought.

NOT YET WHO WE ARE SUPPOSED TO BE

Now, some twenty-nine years later, I am more of a realist. These days, I often feel *more* sinful and *less* holy and virtuous than I did in those first days as a brand-new Christian. Although there are many ways in which I have become more like Christ, in other ways I still ignore and disobey and even deny him.

When I am at my best, those who are closest to me will tell you that the fruit of the Spirit is at work in my life. When I am at my worst, those same people will tell you that I can be petty and even angry about the most insignificant things. I get road rage. I get way too irritated with people who eat a little too loudly. I think about money a lot more than I should. I find more satisfaction in the praise of people than I do in the grace of God. I can be selfish, cowardly, conflict averse, jealous, and ambitious in all the wrong ways. I can, like the Pharisees, use my spiritual gifts and platform as a means to draw attention to myself and applause from others—applause that belongs to God, who alone deserves the glory. Sometimes when an immodest movie scene appears, I don't look away. I am afraid about the future as much as I trust God for it. I am a man who lives by fear as much as I am one who lives by faith.

Because of this, when I see Jesus on the cross crying out, "My God, why have you forsaken me?" I often think, "My God, why *haven't* you forsaken me?" I am with Herman Melville on this one, for like his sailor Ishmael in *Moby Dick*, I am "dreadfully cracked about the head, and sadly need mending."[1] I am now twenty-nine years a Christian and the words of Brennan Manning ring as true now as ever:

> I am a bundle of paradoxes. I believe and I doubt, I hope and get discouraged, I love and I hate, I feel bad about feeling good, I feel guilty about not feeling guilty. I am trusting and suspicious. I am honest and I still play games. Aristotle said I am a rational animal; I say I am an angel with an incredible capacity for beer.[2]

A far cry from the irresistible faith I once thought would describe my life, I sometimes feel like I am more part of the problem than I am part of the solution.

Do you ever feel the same about your own life? Are we hopeless?

Thankfully, there is also plenty of reason *not* to despair. Because of Jesus, encouragement is available to us as we experience the disappointment of anticlimax and as we face the fact that, until Jesus returns, we will continue to fall short of the glory for which we have been created. Encouragement comes from knowing that even the greatest heroes of faith were flawed and broken—wrecked, weary, restless, and sometimes tortured sinners—even when they were at their very best.

The prophet Isaiah, whose lips were skilled at declaring the truth, beauty, and character of God to the people of Israel, had a vision of the holiness of God in the temple. This experience was enough to make God's prophet hang his head in grief. Isaiah became convinced that, in comparison to his Creator, even his purest and most virtuous body part—his prophet and preacher's *mouth*—was flat-out dirty: "Woe is me! For I am lost," the prophet exclaimed, "for I am a man of unclean lips" (Isa. 6:5).

Similarly, the apostle Paul felt the gravity of his own hypocrisy more at the end of his journey than at the beginning. Early on as a Christian, he referred to himself as "Paul, an apostle." Later, he became "Paul, the least of the apostles," then later, "Paul, the least of all the saints," then finally, this: "The saying is trustworthy and deserving of full acceptance, that Christ Jesus came into the world to save sinners, of whom I am the foremost" (1 Tim. 1:15). He also wrote with great emotion about the inner conflict of living inconsistently with his inmost, Spirit-formed desires: "Wretched man that I am! Who will deliver me from this body of death? Thanks be to God through Jesus Christ our Lord!" (Rom. 7:24–25).

There is great paradox to life in Jesus Christ. We are on our way home, but we aren't there yet. We long to be better than we are, but can't quite figure out how to move forward, or even where to begin. The new has come, but the old, fleshly self remains with us. We are being made more like Christ, but our sin and selfishness and narcissism and idolatrous leanings are always there, threatening— even promising—to stunt progress. We move two steps forward then one step back, and sometimes three.

This is our shared fearfully and wonderfully made yet frail human reality. Aren't you relieved that those you respect most in the faith also have shortcomings? Aren't you relieved that so many of the men and women in the Bible—people like Isaiah and Paul, Rahab and Martha—are men and women with deep, abiding flaws? Aren't you relieved that every last one of them is an incomplete work in progress, a person whose least flattering features remained with them until their dying day, even as they journeyed *toward* perfection? How awful and disheartening it would be if the valiant, self-sacrificing, heroic disciples of Jesus weren't also screw-ups just like us. Their failings bring me almost as much comfort as the promises of God, because if there is hope for busted-up sinners like them, then there is also hope for a busted-up sinner like me.

If God shook the earth through the likes of these, then certainly God has the power to shake the earth through the likes of us.

OUR NECESSARY STARTING POINT

The beginning of blessedness—and the beginning of real *change* that will cause the world to notice the light in us—is not the realization that we are okay, but the realization that we are *not* okay. It is not in becoming convinced that we are superior to everyone else, but in recognizing that we are no better than anyone else. It is not in believing that we are strong and capable and competent, but in accepting that we are frail and incapable and weak, while also being fearfully and wonderfully made (Ps. 139:14). It is not in thinking that God expects us to be awesome and prettied-up and all put together, but in gaining confidence that God has first and foremost, in Christ, caused us to be forgiven, loved, faithful, and free. It is from this humble place—and only from this place—that we have any chance of growing into the virtues of Christ. It is only when we can cry out, "God, be merciful to me, a sinner!" that we are sent home justified, blameless in his sight, and confident in his love (Luke 18:9–14).

As my friend the Los Angeles pastor Rankin Wilbourne often observes, God does not love us to the degree that we are *like* Christ. Rather, God loves us to the degree that we are *in* Christ. And that's always 100 percent.

It is essential to begin our journey together with this truth in our minds and hearts—that the first step in becoming like Jesus is acknowledging how unlike Jesus we are and knowing that he loves us just the same. This means that we should not suppress or cover over the doubts we have about ourselves, pretending as if they didn't exist. Rather, we must start listening to those doubts and applying the truth about Jesus to them. We must not try to pull ourselves up by our bootstraps. Rather, we must realize that we don't even have boots. We must not merely think that we have problems. Rather, we must understand that we *are* our own biggest problem, our own worst nightmare, our own worst enemy. As William Shakespeare's Cassius observes, "The fault, dear Brutus, is not in our stars but in ourselves."[3]

Dr. Martyn Lloyd-Jones shares a similar perspective on our human condition: "The first thing you must realize, as you look at that mountain which you are told you must ascend, is that you cannot do it, that you are utterly incapable in and of yourself, and that any attempt to do it in your own strength is proof positive that you have not understood it."[4] God's call on our lives, then, is first and foremost *not* a call to action but a call to brokenness and contrition, for a broken and contrite heart he will not despise (Ps. 51:17).

WE STUMBLE ON

Where do we go from here? As my friend and songwriter Tom Douglas often says, "We stumble on."

This is the paradox: in the midst of our ongoing failure, we nevertheless continue our journey of becoming more like Jesus. The apostle Paul's wish for the first-century Galatians is still our Lord's wish for us today: that Christ be formed in us (Gal. 4:19) and that the fruit of the Spirit—love, joy, peace, patience, kindness, goodness, faithfulness, gentleness, and self-control—become the most dominant, visible, increasing, and operative attributes of our lives (Gal. 5:22–23).

Though we will remain broken and conflicted and beset by sin until our last breath, we cannot allow ourselves to ignore our pursuit of Christ and his Spirit-filled virtues. Even though we will never fully attain it in this life, we must continue to strive with all the energy Christ supplies *toward* the perfection for which we were made—recognizing that even the striving is a gift given to us by him. From beginning to end, our confidence is not in ourselves but in God. He began a good work in us, and he will be faithful to complete it until the day of Christ Jesus (Phil. 1:6). In the same way that he saved us, he will ultimately complete us—by grace, through faith, and in Christ—so that God alone might receive the glory.

I can't think of many better (and strangely admirable) examples of persistent striving to overcome character weakness than the late Samuel Johnson, a Christian and literary giant of the eighteenth century. Johnson struggled for decades against the "deadly sin" of sloth. Here are some excerpts from his diary:

> **The year 1738:** Oh Lord, enable me to redeem the time which I have spent in sloth.
> **1757 (nineteen years later):** O mighty God, enable me to shake off sloth and redeem the time misspent in idleness and sin by diligent application of the days yet remaining.
> **1759:** Enable me to shake off idleness and sloth.
> **1761:** I have resolved until I have resolved that I am afraid to resolve again.
> **1764:** My indolence since my last reception of the sacrament has sunk into grossest sluggishness. My purpose is from this time to avoid idleness and to rise early.

Later in 1764: I resolve to rise early, not later than 6:00 if I can.

1765: I purpose to rise at 8:00 because, though, I shall not rise early it will be much [earlier] than I now rise for I often lie until 2:00.

1769: I am not yet in a state to form any resolutions. I purpose and hope to rise early in the morning, by 8:00, and by degrees, at 6:00.

1775: When I look back upon resolution of improvement and amendments which have, year after year, been made and broken, why do I yet try to resolve again? I try because reformation is necessary, and despair is criminal. [He resolves again to rise at 8:00.]

1781 (three years before his death, forty-three years since his first resolution): I will not despair, help me, oh my God. [He resolves to rise at 8:00 or sooner to avoid idleness.][5]

We are not alone in our failures. Johnson's forty-three years of frustration and failure—much like the sins and setbacks that beset you and me again and again—played a key role in the way God intended to shape and ultimately complete him. In some ways, this place of anticlimax and fumbling is right where God wants us to be. For it is only from this posture that we come to see how much we need the loving-kindness that Jesus is so happy and so ready to give to us. It is only from this posture that we recognize the truth that apart from Jesus Christ, we can do nothing (John 15:5).

And yet, with Jesus Christ, all things are possible. In Samuel Johnson's case, despite decades of losing the battle with laziness and sloth, he became a renowned poet, writer, ethicist, literary expert, and linguist. Significantly, Johnson, who described himself as "a life radically wretched" and filled with "mournful narratives," was one of the most celebrated literary figures of his time—with expertise in poetry, philosophical and political commentary, lexicography, and more. Most notably, in 1775, Johnson published the first *Dictionary of the English Language*, later earning him the nickname "Dictionary Johnson."[6]

As my wife often says, every single person except for Jesus is a mixed bag. This includes the likes of Samuel Johnson, who fiercely struggled all the days of his life with his own shortcomings, failures, and sins, and yet whose life was by no means wasted. Even *during* his years of deepest struggle and self-doubt, Johnson was leaving the world better than he had found it—laboring and serving from the light that had been placed in him by God.

TO ERR IS NOT HUMAN AFTER ALL

There is another reason we should be encouraged even as we struggle with our snail-pace progress. Last I checked, there were 861,000 self-help books available on Amazon. The sheer popularity of self-help books points to the reality that humans live with an insatiable longing for something more, something better. This is why we keep making resolutions every New Year's even though, like Samuel Johnson, we will almost certainly not follow through with them. We are plagued with an inevitable frustration. We were made for more and we know it. As we are reminded in Paul's letter to the Romans, we groan under the weight of this longing (Rom. 8:22–24). When the light of God is active within us, this frustration can be a hopeful sign of what's to come but has not yet been realized. Call it a holy dissatisfaction, a frustrated anticipation of what we know will one day come true: that we will be like Jesus Christ, for we will see him as he is (1 John 3:2–3).

Our innate, unshakable longing to be *better* suggests that, deep down, we don't really believe that to err is human after all. If we are governed by Scripture, filled with the Holy Spirit, and aware of our calling to become perfect as our heavenly Father is perfect, we will always feel a tension with that assertion. The very fact that we confess our sins betrays the idea. As those who are created in the image of God, we are hardwired to long for more. As Blaise Pascal has written:

> The greatness of man is so evident, that it is even proved by his wretchedness. For what in animals is nature we call in man wretchedness; by which we recognize that, his nature being like that of animals, he has fallen from a better nature which once was his.
>
> For who is unhappy at not being a king, except a deposed king?[7]

Put more simply, the same impulse that kept Samuel Johnson from giving up on his own sanctification should also be an impulse that drives us. We are meant to grow. We are meant to improve. We are meant to become unstuck. But the question remains: How?

FORGIVEN, PERFECT, AND LOVED IN GOD'S SIGHT

When the apostle Paul taught about how Christians grow in becoming more like Jesus, he began with hopeful words: "Walk by the Spirit, and you will not gratify the desires of the flesh. For the desires of the flesh are against the Spirit, and the desires of the Spirit are against the flesh, for these are opposed to each other, to keep you from doing the things you want to do. But if you are led by the Spirit, you are not under the law" (Gal. 5:16–18). This last phrase is worth examining closely, because understanding it is essential to understanding how we grow.

You are not under the law. Wonderfully and profoundly, this statement declares that we are no longer under the ominous threat of God's judgment. On the cross, Jesus took the punishment that our sins deserve, thereby moving our judgment day from the future to the past. It's no wonder that the same chapter that begins with the declaration that there is no condemnation in Christ (Rom. 8:1–2) goes on to explain why the most repeated command in Scripture is "Do not fear." Surrounded by the realities of tribulation, distress, persecution, famine, nakedness, and sword, Paul nonetheless asserts that if God is for us, none can be against us. And God—who gave up his Son for us all—is surely for us, so much so that nothing in all creation will ever be able to separate us from his love in Christ (Rom. 8:31–39).

Being in Jesus and not under law also means we are considered *perfect* in God's eyes. We have nothing left to prove. The impeccable, perfectly virtuous life of Jesus Christ—*his* love, *his* joy, *his* peace, *his* patience, *his* kindness, *his* faithfulness, *his* gentleness, and *his* self-control—was forever credited to us at the cross. "For our sake [God] made him to be sin who knew no sin, so that in him we might become the righteousness of God" (2 Cor. 5:21). No pedigrees or pedestals necessary. Through faith, we are blameless in God's eyes, positionally perfect, not because of our goodness but because of his.

And it keeps getting better. In Jesus, we are also *loved* by God in the longest, widest, highest, and deepest ways, such that nothing can ever separate us from that love—not even ourselves (Rom. 8:31–39). Therefore, we have nothing left to hide. We can strip off our religious masks, forsake the impostor/poseur, and start living our lives freely again, "naked and unashamed" before the eyes of our Judge who has now become our Savior. With our lives bound up in the finished work of Jesus, we are the recipients of God's blessing pronounced over him at his baptism: beloved daughters and sons with whom the Father is well pleased. In Jesus, the Father has no punitive anger left for us. In Jesus, the Father takes great delight in us, quiets us with his love, and rejoices over us with love songs (Zeph. 3:17). In Jesus, the Father invites us to address him intimately. He is our *Abba*, meaning "Daddy" or "Papa."

We are now, through the finished work of Jesus, invited to assume the identity that God has given us. Or as Catholic writer Brennan Manning put it, "Define yourself radically as one beloved by God. This is the true self. Every other identity is an illusion."[8] While we are simultaneously sinners and saints, in Christ we are identified solely as the latter. We are fully known and fully loved. We are found out and never rejected. Nothing in all creation can change this.

For the Christian, the work is finished. As a child of God in Christ, you are no longer a slave to a wearying religion or a hollow philosophy that says you must earn God's approval through willpower and moral resolve. The burden is not on you to become your own (or anyone else's) savior. The pressure is off! Instead, you are set free by the assurance that God's heart is already in your hands, even as he is eager for you to put your heart entirely into his. "Come to me, all who labor and are heavy laden," Jesus said, "and I will give you rest" (Matt. 11:28). What could possibly be more freeing than this? And this freedom is what enables us to grow into Christians who make an irresistible mark on the world.

THE POWER AND PROCESS FOR CHANGE

When you become a Christian, your new and favored position in God's eyes is based on the finished work of Jesus on your behalf and nothing else. This reality is also the power for change. Having been declared forgiven, perfect, and loved in God's sight, you are free to pursue obedience to God's law. You pursue obedience not as a way to earn his favor but to start becoming the healthiest, most alive version of yourself—to become the person *you already are* in the sight of God.

When you become a Christian, God's law assumes a new dimension and role for you. Instead of operating as a constraining influence from outside of you, his law now operates as a guiding influence from within you. His law is no longer an indictment that condemns you or a bar set so high that it only crushes you. Rather, because you are a forgiven and favored child of God, the law is now to you like water to a fish. It is the healthiest, most liberating habitat for you as one created in the image of God. It is your roadmap for growing into the name you have already been given—"holy and blameless before him" (Eph. 1:4). As a child of God, you are free to "grow into God's law" like a small boy might grow over time into the extra-large shirt given to him at birth by his father.

This process of growing into the forgiveness, perfect righteousness, love, and character of Jesus is precisely that—*a process*. This is why the apostle Paul chose a botanical metaphor to help us understand what growth looks like and how it progresses (Gal. 5:22–23). Fruit never sprouts up instantly into its fully developed, ripened, juicy, sweet, and most edible state. Rather, fruit grows over time through a slow, ordinary, God-orchestrated process.

Like an apple or an orange, spiritual fruit grows in spurts and seasons. During the "off" seasons, it may even appear that the tree has died because its leaves have fallen and it is not bearing fruit. But in reality, the tree is not dead but merely dormant. Though it may appear lifeless and fruitless, it is actually preparing for the next fruit-bearing season. So it is with life in Christ. The *signs* of life may disappear for a time (as they did, for example, with Peter when he was denying Christ, or with Thomas when he refused to believe[9]), but *life* is still there. As was the case for Peter and Thomas, and as is the case for every fruit tree, true Christians who find themselves in a dormant season will most certainly return to bearing fruit again. This is their truest nature.

Also, like an apple or an orange, the Spirit's fruit tends to grow gradually rather than immediately. Have you ever witnessed a plant growing before your eyes in real time? Of course not! Although growth cannot be seen in real time, it becomes visible in retrospect. So it is with the fruit of the Spirit. What was once a seed is now a sprout. What was once a sprout is now a small tree. What was once a small tree is now a large, fruit-bearing tree. What used to be a large, fruit-bearing tree is now an orchard.

When I was first starting out as a pastor, I had a very hard time receiving any kind of criticism. Even the slightest correction from a congregant, friend, or family member would send me into an emotional tailspin. When the criticisms were accurate, I would experience self-loathing. When I felt that the criticisms were inaccurate or unfair, I would become defensive and even resentful. Even though I often taught and preached on passages like Matthew 18 and Galatians 6 and Psalm 141—all of which encourage the gentle giving and humble receiving of constructive feedback—I responded like a functional atheist when it was time to apply the teaching to my own life. One Sunday, I could preach to our church that if someone sins against you, "go and tell him his fault" (Matt. 18:15), and "faithful are the wounds of a friend" (Prov. 27:6). Then on Monday, a fellow staff member or my wife or somebody else could apply my teaching by showing *me* a fault of *mine*, and my inner pit bull would come out.

That was twenty years ago. Since that time, the Holy Spirit has gradually shown me how destructive it is to respond to critique with self-loathing or with contempt. In fact, many of my most significant seasons of growth have occurred as a result of a conversation that began with, "Scott, we need to talk about how you have hurt me," or "Scott, I am seeing a pattern in your speech [or behavior] that is beginning to concern me," or "Scott, you aren't practicing what you preach."

This is the place where some may ask, "What about when the critique is unfair?" "What if it is clear that the person is out to get you, is twisting your words, is just trying to pick a fight . . . ?" These are legitimate questions.

As my friend and leadership expert Carey Nieuwhof has said, "Don't wrestle with pigs, because you will both get dirty. And the difference between you and the pig is that the pig will enjoy it." Of course, Carey is not insinuating that we should refer to our fellow human beings as pigs. He is simply, and rightly, suggesting that engaging people who seem to be out to get you or just looking for something to be offended by (which seems more common now than ever) will be counterproductive more times than not.

Not long ago, I was tested by such a criticism when a stranger retweeted something I said on Twitter and then publicly attributed to me motives that I did not have. He twisted my words and then went in for the kill with a "Gotcha!" question.

Twenty years earlier, I would have become defensive and fired back with an insult or "Gotcha!" question of my own. But this time, I went to my critic's Twitter profile to see what I could learn about him. It turned out that he was unemployed, recently divorced, and a single father of young children. While these factors do not justify attacking a stranger on social media, they provided a context from which I could process and respond to his behavior toward me.

Very quickly, my feelings toward this man changed from anger and defensiveness to empathy. As I often remind our congregation in sermons, "Hurting people hurt people." My social media critic was no exception to this. So instead of retaliating with an insult or two of my own, I made a financial donation to a GoFundMe link that some of his own social media followers had initiated to help him through the hard season in which he found himself.

I tell this story not because I think I am the best example of how to respond to criticism. Those who know me best would tell you that I am not. But what I hope you can see here is that, over time, the Holy Spirit *can* change hearts and behaviors—even opening doors for enemies to become friends, or at least to become empathetic toward one another, with gentle answers that can turn away wrath, as opposed to harsh and retaliatory words that only stir up *more* division and anger (Prov. 15:1).

When Christ invites us to come to him as we are, he doesn't intend for us to *stay* as we are. His influence, though gradual and sometimes slow, is meant to transform us. For if anyone is in Christ, he is a new creation. The old has gone and the new has come (2 Cor. 5:17). A slow rate of change need not lead to self-loathing, because even when sin abounds for the Christian, the grace of God "super-abounds" (Rom. 5:20).

BELONGING AND ABIDING

As we allow Jesus to set the pace of our spiritual transformation, we can take the pressure off ourselves to "get there, and fast" in the journey toward becoming like Jesus Christ. Why? Because God *cannot* love us more than he already does in Christ, and he *will not* love us less.[10]

God is always more patient with us than we are with ourselves. If only we could see ourselves in the way that he sees us—as ones whose imperfections and sins have been completely covered in Christ and who are loved by him on our worst day as much as we are on our best. If only we could believe that God is even more prone to forgive than we are prone to sin—that where our sin abounds, his grace abounds all the more (Rom. 5:20). Then we could start loathing ourselves less and loving ourselves more. We could become more hopeful about God's promise to complete the work that he began in us.

The beloved status God has imparted to us provides the motivation and the emotional resources for us to become "mature in Christ . . . struggling with all his energy that he powerfully works within [us]" (Col. 1:28–29). Our beloved status is also the context in which we can contemplate the apostle Peter's compelling—and challenging—vision for growth:

> His divine power has granted to us all things that pertain to life and godliness, through the knowledge of him who called us to his own glory and excellence, by which he has granted to us his precious and very great promises, so that through them you may become partakers of the divine nature, having escaped from the corruption that is in the world because of sinful desire. For this very reason, make every effort to supplement your faith with virtue, and virtue with knowledge, and knowledge with self-control, and self-control with steadfastness, and steadfastness with godliness, and godliness with brotherly affection, and brotherly affection with love. (2 Peter 1:3–7)

The question is, what is our role in all of this? How are we supposed to meaningfully *participate* in our own journey to become like Jesus Christ? If God is ultimately the one who completes the work he has begun in us, what are *we* to do and how are *we* to contribute to the process?

We find our answers by considering how Jesus taught and sent out his first disciples.

As Jesus was about to send his disciples out to love the world, what did he do first? He gathered them together to be with him and fed them a meal. Then he showed them the full extent of his love by getting down on his knees and washing their feet. Only after this did Jesus, the King who became a servant *to* his servants, tell them that they, too, should wash one another's feet (John 13:1–17). Having been loved by him, they could now love others. Having spent time with Jesus—not only for this meal but for three solid years—they could now be like him.

Because Jesus is this kind of friend to us—"washing our feet" from every direction, every day of our lives—we now have the resources to become, over time, better human beings. The closer we grow to Jesus, the less dominated by sin we will be. And the less we are dominated by sin, the more like Jesus we will become. We will no longer be dormant but growing, healthy, life-giving, fruit-bearing trees that feed and nourish the world.

We ask, "What are we to do?" and we find that we participate in becoming *like* Jesus as we invest ourselves in being *with* Jesus. We begin to assume his likeness, not by scurrying about getting busy for Jesus as Martha did, but by sitting at his feet as Mary did (Luke 10:38–42).

"But how *do* we sit at Jesus' feet? How *do* we draw near to him and be with him that we may become like him?" the pragmatist in us still asks.

To these questions, Jesus says we must seek first the kingdom of God. When we do, "all these things"—including Christlike character—will be added to us. We seek his kingdom chiefly through the means of *abiding* in Christ and his Word, the subject of our next chapter.

CHAPTER 2

GETTING OUR HEADS STRAIGHT

SOMETIMES I STRUGGLE WITH THE BIBLE.

Some of my struggle has to do with focus. When I read Scripture, distractions abound. So many things feel more urgent and alluring—things like email, text messages, social media, the day's news cycle, to-do lists, the latest Netflix series or music release, and opportunities to connect with actual, in-the-flesh human beings, to name just a few.

Boredom can set in. True, it is all God's Word—what an amazing gift! But when it comes to plodding through Leviticus or those long lists of who begat whom and who is in this tribe or that tribe, or trying to make sense of laws that feel dated, or engaging the darker components of Scripture—rape, incest, family dysfunction, bloody wars, lying and stealing, backbiting, pettiness, and frustrated prayers—part of me thinks there might be a better use of time.

I also find the Bible perplexing. In the pages of Scripture, children sometimes die for the sins of their parents. Entire people groups are oppressed and abused and enslaved by people in power.

Weak and innocent people suffer, and hurtful, mean-hearted people prosper. God saves some and passes over others. Two well-meaning men get struck dead for touching the ark of God. And the list goes on. These and other unnerving depictions can feel less like a source of inspiration and more like a dark and twisted cable channel.

Yes, I am a Christian minister—a *Bible* guy—who sometimes struggles with what he sees in the Bible. It comforts me that I am not alone in this. Even one of my personal heroes, C. S. Lewis, dealt with similar feelings about the Bible. Reflecting on Psalm 19:10, where King David likens Scripture to a treasure of fine gold and a taste sweeter than honey, Lewis wrote:

> This was to me at first very mysterious. "Thou shalt not steal, thou shalt not commit adultery"—I can understand that a man can, and must, respect these "statutes," and try to obey them, and assent to them in his heart. But it is very hard to find how they could be, so to speak, delicious, how they exhilarate. . . . They may obey, they may still respect the statute. But surely it could be more aptly compared to the dentist's forceps or the front line than to anything enjoyable and sweet.[1]

Indeed, honest Bible readers, even skilled and imaginative teachers of the Bible like C. S. Lewis, have found parts of it difficult, puzzling, mystifying, and even offensive. And if this is indeed the case—that even ministers and teachers of the Bible struggle—how can we expect people *outside* Christianity to find our faith, which is based *upon* that very same Bible, to be irresistible?

Just as there are many reasons to rejoice in, get inspired by, and take comfort in certain parts of the Bible, there are other reasons the Bible might disturb us—especially those parts that contradict our feelings, hopes, dreams, expectations, traditions, and cultural values. This reality is what gave birth to the idea that people don't reject the Bible because it contradicts itself; they reject the Bible because it contradicts them.

The apostle Paul, whose life was completely upended when the Word of God came to him on the road to Damascus, would later write such things as these:

> All Scripture is breathed out by God and profitable for teaching, for reproof, for correction, and for training in righteousness, that the man of God may be complete, equipped for every good work. (2 Tim. 3:16–17)

> We destroy arguments and every lofty opinion raised against the knowledge of God, and take every thought captive to obey Christ. (2 Cor. 10:5)

> Do not be conformed to this world, but be transformed by the renewal of your mind, that by testing you may discern what is the will of God, what is good and acceptable and perfect. (Rom. 12:2)

Jesus, too, emphasized the centrality of God's Word in the lives of believers when he said that we must love God not only with our hearts but also with our minds (Luke 10:27). He described the revealed will of his Father as his own food and drink (John 4:34); resisted Satan's temptations by quoting Scripture, saying, "Man shall not live by bread alone, but by every word that comes from the mouth of God" (Matt. 4:4); quoted the Psalms as he died on the cross (Matt. 27:46; Luke 23:46); and emphasized to his followers that abiding in him and abiding in Scripture are one and the same (John 15:7–10).

In other words, following Jesus and following Scripture are

inseparable endeavors. Whatever we may think about the Bible, we simply cannot separate life in Christ from a life in which Scripture dominates our thoughts, beliefs, words, and actions. Fulfilling our calling to love and enjoy God with everything we are and to love our neighbor as ourselves—that is, becoming irresistible—stands or falls on whether or not we become people of the Book.

The Bible is not *merely* perplexing as a book. It is also life-giving. In fact, aligning our beliefs, words, and lives with the Bible is an essential ingredient for irresistible faith. When such alignment occurs, we become like fruit-bearing trees in the world, whose health and vitality are seen by what they produce. The signs of our alignment with the Bible—love, joy, peace, patience, kindness, goodness, faithfulness, gentleness, and self-control (see the fruit of the Spirit of Gal. 5:22–23 and the love attributes of 1 Cor. 13:4–8)—multiply as our alignment deepens. We become the type of people who work hard and rest well, who honor our parents and others in authority over us, who are faithful in marriage and sexually chaste in singleness, who resist the urge to take what is not ours, who live content with what we have been given, and who don't bear false witness against others through gossip or slander or spin (the Ten Commandments of Ex. 20:1–17).

And who in the world wouldn't want friends, neighbors, and colleagues like that?

THE HOLY SPIRIT'S ROLE

And yet, we cannot muster up love for God's Word or surrender to it on our own. There first must be a divine action—an action we are unable to manage or control—that occurs for the Bible to become sweet to us. We must be acted *upon* from the outside to become a renewed and transformed people with an irresistible faith.

We know from Scripture that God's words contain immense power. His spoken word brought dead people back to life (John 11:1–44), stilled violent storms at sea (Mark 4:35–41), banished evil spirits (Luke 8:26–39), and caused water and earth and sky and galaxies to come into being (Gen. 1).

And yet, God's breathed-out Word will have no impact upon us until God breathes life *into* us. Just as a rocket cannot launch or a car cannot travel without an igniting force to fire up its engine, so a Christian cannot be transformed by the Bible without the prerequisite new birth through the Holy Spirit: "Unless one is born of water and the Spirit, he cannot enter the kingdom of God" (John 3:5).

What was true of Jesus' disciples is also true of us: Before we can do anything to love God or neighbor, we must receive a power from on high (Luke 24:49; Acts 2:1–13). Consequently, our prayers must include the humble request that God "take not" his Holy Spirit from us (Ps. 51:11) but instead give us the Holy Spirit in increasing measure (2 Kings 2:9; Luke 11:13).

Among other things, the filling of the Spirit creates in us a new posture toward the Bible. Rather than being bored and unmoved by it, we become drawn to it. Rather than being perplexed by it, we become driven with desire to know and understand more deeply. In fact, a sure sign that we *have* been filled with the Holy Spirit is the presence of a new affection and thirst for Scripture. God promises his people a new heart or spiritual "flesh" to animate our otherwise dead spiritual "bones" (Jer. 31:31–34; Ezek. 36:26–27; Eph. 2:1–10). In the words of the great theologian Benjamin B. Warfield:

> The Holy Spirit, when applying the benefits of Christ's redemption, saving men from the guilt and dominion of sin, works *by and with the Word of God*. . . . The Holy Spirit, the indwelling

God, by and with the Word, creates an experience conformed to the Word, and so, honoring and confirming it, testifies that it is the Word of God.[2]

As the Holy Spirit lives in our hearts by faith, we humbly and even joyfully accept that God's thoughts are higher than our thoughts, and his ways higher than our ways (Isa. 55:9). The Bible, as opposed to our feelings, opinions, experiences, and wishes, begins to have the final say about things that are true, beautiful, and praiseworthy. Where Scripture affirms us and where it contradicts us, where Scripture delights us and where it offends us, where Scripture comforts us and where it stings us, where Scripture clarifies and where it confuses us—every word, sentence, paragraph, and punctuation mark becomes a revered and cherished portion of God's direct and shaping authority that is relevant to all people of all cultures and all times.

We creatures are not meant to censor our Creator's words; his words are meant to censor us. We are not meant to revise his insights; his insights are meant to revise us. We are not meant to realign his statutes with our sensibilities; his statutes are meant to realign us with his sensibilities. We are not meant to improve upon his Word; his Word is meant to improve us. When the Holy Spirit convinces our hearts of these things, the authority of the whole Christ, the whole Scripture, the whole time becomes our guiding principle. The Bible becomes to us "the only infallible rule of faith and practice."[3]

AN ACQUIRED TASTE

For those who claim Jesus as Savior and Lord, the Bible in all of its parts is a reliable roadmap for trusting, following, and becoming like him. It points us to the path of human flourishing, to life as our Creator intended it to be. It paves the road for us so that we can pursue our ultimate purpose of loving God fully and loving neighbors deeply, not according to our own wisdom and instincts but according to his revealed will and purpose for our lives.

If we have a lingering, unshakable distaste for the Bible—for *any* part of it—the problem lies not with the Bible but with the taste buds of our souls. It does not point to a deficit in God or in his Word but to a deficit in us, a vulnerability that tempts us to call evil "good" or to call good "evil" (Isa. 5:20). But when the taste buds of our souls become aligned with the Holy Spirit and God's Word, when the palate of our souls has been properly cleansed, even the seemingly bland and difficult and disorienting parts of the Bible will become sweet to us. Our response to Scripture, even to the hard and perplexing parts, will resemble that of the prophet Ezekiel.

God commanded Ezekiel, who has often been spoken of as "the prophet of doom," to eat a scroll containing God's "words of lamentation and mourning and woe" (Ezek. 2:10). Sounds like a party or like the sermon you don't want to miss, doesn't it? Yet Ezekiel's reaction, after obeying that curious invitation to *eat* and then digest God's more difficult, bothersome words, was remarkable:

"Then I ate it, and it was in my mouth as sweet as honey" (Ezek. 3:3).

Even the hard parts became *as sweet as honey* to the taste buds of Ezekiel's biblically formed, Holy Spirit-animated, God-oriented soul. God had given him a new heart and had put spiritual flesh on his otherwise unresponsive spiritual bones. When God did this, the prophet was suddenly able to see things as they truly are. The blinders were lifted, and the whole Word of God—even God's words of lamentation and mourning and woe—not only made sense, but became delicious to him.

As the saying goes, we should let our religion be less of a theory and more of a love affair.[4] Anyone who falls in love knows that love embraces all of the beloved and not just parts of her or him. A true love affair includes a lasting covenant to have and to hold, for better and for worse, in joy and in sorrow, in sickness and in health, as long as both lovers shall live. It includes giving our whole self to our beloved, and also receiving our beloved's whole self into our own heart and life. This is how God loves us. He comes to us in the person of Jesus and pledges his whole self to us, promising to love us fully and forever as a husband to his bride. In return, he wants us to give our whole selves to him, "forsaking all others," until his every word becomes our happy wish. As the ancient hymn puts it, "To see the Law by Christ fulfilled, to hear his pardoning voice, turns the slave into a child and duty into choice."[5]

Just as parents want their children to eat vegetables and not just cake, our Father in heaven—who always knows us better than we know ourselves and loves us more than we love ourselves—wants us to "eat" all of his words rather than only some of them. God's love, forgiveness, salvation, and eternal promises taste delicious to our souls. These are like a tasty main course and dessert at dinnertime. But there are other "menu items" in the diet his Word prescribes for us—things like being generous with our money, forgiving those who have injured us, limiting our sexual activity to marriage, committing ourselves to a local church, preferring servanthood over selfishness, and denying ourselves daily—that may seem more like raw vegetables to a child. Admittedly, our taste for these biblical truths might be more acquired than natural. Yet we must not childishly shove the "vegetables" off our plates. We should keep eating them faithfully until we acquire a new taste, until every one of God's words becomes delicious, as sweet as honey, to the taste buds of our souls. Just as a steady diet of vegetables and consistent exercise nurture healthy, solid bodies, so a steady diet of God-inspired words, aided and animated by the Holy Spirit, nurtures healthy, solid souls. And where it seems more difficult to acquire such a taste, we must remember Jesus' invitation: "How much more will the heavenly Father give the Holy Spirit to those who ask him!" (Luke 11:13).

When God's Word becomes our chief guiding reality, when we abide in Jesus Christ by abiding in his Word, when we agree with our Savior that "man shall not live by bread alone, but by every word that comes from the mouth of God" (Matt. 4:4), we become positioned by God to live more beautiful, more compelling, more irresistible lives. As evidence of this, look no further than Jesus, who lived perfectly in accord with his Father's word and continues to compel the world's attention today.

As we become people of the Book, we position ourselves to abide in Jesus. Our souls receive nourishment from Scripture, just as fruit-bearing branches do from the vine that supports them (John 15:7–10). Word-centered disciples, Bible-saturated sojourners, sinner-saints formed by the Old and New Testaments, who live by every word that proceeds from the mouth of God (Matt. 4:4), are the people God means for us to be. He aims to make us into faithful men and women, consciously beloved and graced servants of Jesus, eager to leave people, places, and things in a better condition than we found them.

THINKING WELL

Saturating our minds with the Bible's truths and promises—or what theologian Cornelius Van Til called "thinking God's thoughts after him"[6]—makes us wiser and builds up our ability to see God, people, the world, and ourselves with accuracy and clarity. In a world where truth is seen as relative, and amid all the confusion, disagreement, and uncertainty that results, it is all the more paramount to have our views about truth shaped by a universal, infallible source outside ourselves—namely our Creator, who, as Francis Schaeffer once noted, "is there and is not silent."[7] As the psalmist writes, "I have more understanding than all my teachers, for your testimonies are my meditation" (Ps. 119:99).

As noted earlier, the vast majority of Ivy League universities were founded by Christians with an irresistible faith. One such leader was former Princeton president Jonathan Edwards, hailed by *Encyclopedia Britannica* as being among the greatest American philosophers.[8] According to Tim Keller, the secret to Edwards's genius is that if you poked Jonathan Edwards with a fork, he would bleed Bible.

Tim Keller is a pastor and thought leader whom God has used to shape an entire generation of urban, gospel-centered church leaders. While working alongside Tim for five years in New York City, I had the privilege of observing some of the daily practices that shaped him into such a formidable influencer. In addition to a deep life of private prayer, Tim engages in a daily habit of filling his mind and heart with biblical stories, promises, and teachings. For decades, Tim has prayed through every psalm once per month and read through every book of the Bible once per year. As with Edwards, so with Keller. Poke the man with a fork, and he will bleed Bible.

A bright mind from the past is the Puritan John Bunyan, who authored *The Pilgrim's Progress* while imprisoned for his faith. This allegory of life in Christ would later be hailed as a literary masterpiece, as well as a source of deep encouragement for millions. Unlike most of the Puritans, Bunyan had very little formal education. And yet, equipped with a deep practical knowledge of Scripture, he has been marked in history as one of the brightest Christian thought leaders.

The impact of a mind saturated with Scripture is seen not only in the lives of well-known individuals but also through millions of lesser-known men and women shaped by Scripture. For example, consider Timothy's mother and grandmother, who instilled in him a love for Scripture from infancy (2 Tim. 1:5). There was Edward Kimball, a shoe salesman who led Dwight Moody to Christ by sharing with him the Bible's basic truths of salvation by grace through faith. There was a small-town church deacon who did the same for Charles Spurgeon. And there is the father of a friend of mine, a businessman and faithful, exemplary Bible teacher in his local church. When asked one Sunday what it would take to be able to teach the Bible and pray as thoughtfully, accurately, and compellingly as he did, he answered, "Read the Bible every day for twenty-five years."

There is great intellectual benefit to gaining biblical knowledge. Countless literary masterpieces—from Charles Dickens, Fyodor Dostoevsky, Jane Austen, William Faulkner, Marilynne Robinson, Toni Morrison, John Steinbeck, Leo Tolstoy, Flannery O'Connor, and J. R. R. Tolkien, to name a paltry few—are laced with biblical references, allusions, and insights.

Similarly, musical contributions from the likes of George Frideric Handel, John Coltrane, Anne Steele, Johnny Cash, Bob Dylan, Emmylou Harris, Kanye West, Lauryn Hill, and U2 are also saturated with the language of God. We could add to the list the ingenious rhetoric of Martin Luther King Jr., the timeless plays of William Shakespeare, the groundbreaking science of Francis Collins, the insightful political commentary of *New York Times* columnist David Brooks, and many others!

But there is something more than achievement to be had by steeping oneself in the Bible. To the degree we faithfully engage Scripture, we will gain insight that makes us wiser even than our teachers. Ingesting the words of God will make us more intelligent, more insightful, more thoughtful, and more fruitful contributors to God's world.

REJOICING WELL

Besides being one of history's greatest intellects, Jonathan Edwards was also a man of great and irresistible passion and joy. So enamored was Edwards with the truth and beauty of God and Scripture, so filled was he with the Holy Spirit, that he wrote an entire volume titled *Religious Affections*. For Edwards, theology was not doing its full work until it caught fire in the heart, ravished the senses, and captivated the imagination. This is what he meant by "affections." For Edwards, a mere academic knowledge of Scripture made people doctrinaire rather than faithfully doctrinal, leading to puffed-up heads and loveless hearts (1 Cor. 8:1). In his thinking, doctrine isn't truly biblical until it is recognized as beautiful, and we haven't come to truly know God until we have also come to enjoy him. For Edwards, the key to an irresistible faith was an irresistible Christ, found on the pages of an irresistible Bible.

We can observe this prevailing reality for Edwards in this reflection on an experience he had in the woods:

> Once, as I rode out into the woods for my health, in 1737, having alighted from my horse in a retired place, as my manner commonly has been, to walk for divine contemplation and prayer, I had a view, that for me was extraordinary, of the glory of the Son of God, as Mediator between God and man, and his wonderful, great, full, pure and sweet grace and love, and meek and gentle condescension. This grace that appeared so calm and sweet, appeared also great above the heavens. The person of Christ appeared ineffably excellent, with an excellency great

enough to swallow up all thought and conception—which continued, as near as I can judge, about an hour; which kept me the greater part of the time in a flood of tears and weeping aloud. I felt an ardency of soul to be, what I know not otherwise how to express, emptied and annihilated; to lie in the dust, and to be full of Christ alone; to love him with a holy and pure love; to trust in him; to live upon him; to serve and follow him; and to be perfectly sanctified and made pure, with a divine and heavenly purity. I have several other times had views very much of the same nature, and which have had the same effects.[9]

My own handful of "mountaintop" spiritual experiences—ones that have caused me to feel ready to burst out of my skin with Spirit-filled joy—have always, as with Edwards, originated from Scripture-informed *content*. These truths have been embedded into my conscious and subconscious over the course of years—truths about God's attributes and God's world and God's grace and redemption and freedom. Through ordinary, daily Bible reading, when I felt like reading and also when I didn't feel like reading but did it anyway, my mind has been shaped and renewed.

We cannot predict how or when the Holy Spirit will overcome us. As Jesus taught us, the Spirit moves like the wind and we can't predict his mysterious activity (John 3:6–8). But when he *does* decide to move, his action on our hearts always occurs by and with the Word of God, which refers to itself as "the sword of the Spirit" (Eph. 6:17). The Holy Spirit is always aligned with Scripture and is never incongruent with it.

Perhaps this is why the apostle Paul said that he would rather hear five *intelligible* words of God's truth than ten thousand words in a tongue (1 Cor. 14:19). According to Paul, whatever joy and ecstasy can be derived from supernatural experiences like speaking in tongues, none can compare with the more "extraordinary view" described by Jonathan Edwards, in which deep emotion and extraordinary passion for the things of God start with a transformation by the renewing of our minds (Rom. 12:1–2) through His Word.

SUFFERING WELL

There is another extraordinary gift that the Holy Spirit, working by and with the Scriptures, can bring about in our hearts. It is a joy, confidence, and poise independent of circumstances that shows up even—and sometimes especially—in suffering.

Over the years, I have walked alongside men and women who faced death with bitterness and despair. I have also walked alongside men and women who faced death with a settled peace in their hearts, joy on their faces, and certainty that their best days were still ahead of them. It is this latter group whose faith I have found to be irresistible, and whose faith I hope will also sustain me when my time to suffer comes.

At the church in Nashville where I serve as pastor, scores of people have endured deep sorrow and loss, and they have done so exceptionally well. These men and women have not denied suffering or somehow swept its awfulness under the rug. On the contrary, they have looked suffering squarely in the face as sober-minded, hope-filled realists, and have said with the apostle Paul, "'O death, where is your victory? O death, where is your sting?'" (1 Cor. 15:55). They have been sustained by the same conviction that sustained Paul through his trials and tribulations, that in Christ "we are more than conquerors through him who loved us. For I am sure that neither death nor life, nor angels nor rulers, nor things present nor things to come, nor powers, nor height nor depth, nor anything else in all creation, will be able to separate us from the love of God in Christ Jesus our Lord" (Rom. 8:37–39).

One such person was a man from our church named John. John lived a full and beautiful life as a faithful husband, loving father, true friend, gifted artist, and devoted servant of our church. At an age that seemed far too young, John was diagnosed with ALS, a condition that incapacitated him physically, confined him to a wheelchair and breathing machines, and eventually took his life. I would sometimes visit John in his home during his months of decline. For me, these times with John gave new meaning to Paul's reflection on his own suffering. Although the "outer self" may have been wasting away, the "inner self" was being renewed day by day (2 Cor. 4:16).

John did not give in to despair as his body withered from disease. Rather, he faced his situation with remarkable joy, thankfulness, and poise. Though frustrated by the pains and losses associated with his disease, he didn't allow himself to be defined by them. Though he was in great pain, John never grew cynical. When he ate through a straw and food dripped down the side of his face, instead of cursing he would crack a joke. When his nurses and helpers arrived to treat his physical needs, instead of demanding that they do this or that, he invited them to join him for Bible study. When we went to his home to pastor him, he would end up pastoring us.

John's attitude and lightness of being, especially considering the suffering he had been given to endure, made such an impression on me that I finally asked him how he could face suffering with such an admirable poise. His simple and immediate answer was, "Well, that's easy. I've been a Bible reader all of my life. Somewhere along the way, I guess it all sank in."

When John said these words, I found new meaning to the old

saying, "A Bible that's falling apart usually belongs to someone who isn't."

Another man from our church whose name is Al was diagnosed with terminal cancer. Also young in years, Al faced his devastating news and the decline that would follow in a way very similar to John. I will never forget the day he and his wife, Renee, got the news. A couple of other pastors and I visited them that evening, and we were astounded by what Al said. "When I first heard the news," Al told us, "I wanted to ask, 'Why me?' But then it seemed that the better question to ask was, 'Why *not* me?' The Bible says that God loves to manifest his power through our weakness. So I suppose that cancer will be an opportunity for his power to be manifested through me."

On my second visit with Al, he was wearing a pair of brightly colored striped socks. When I asked him about them, he told me they were his "happy socks," which he wore as a constant reminder of what is true . . . that God is a healer, and death and sorrow and sickness cannot and will not ultimately win. How does Al know this? What is the basis for his confidence that even terminal cancer, as the apostle Paul would say, is a "light momentary affliction" in comparison to the everlasting glory and health awaiting every single one of God's children (2 Cor. 4:17–18)?

There's a hymn that we sing regularly at our church, a famous hymn written by Horatio Spafford, a Chicago lawyer and business-man who, along with his wife, suffered the loss of a son to scarlet fever and then all four of their daughters to an accident at sea. After receiving the news that he and his wife were now childless, Spafford penned these words to "It Is Well with My Soul":

> *When peace like a river attendeth my way,*
> *When sorrows like sea billows roll,*
> *Whatever my lot, thou hast taught me to say,*

It is well, it is well with my soul.
Though Satan should buffet and trials should come,
Let this blessed assurance control:
That Christ has regarded my helpless estate
And has shed his own blood for my soul.

Whenever we sing this Scripture-rich hymn at church, I look around to see how it is impacting our people. Almost without fail, those who sing the hymn with the most gusto are the sufferers. This includes people like John with his ALS, Al with his cancer, Jan and Susan with their cancer, Sarah with her chronic fatigue, scores of men and women with their anxiety and depression, and the dozen or so mothers and fathers who, like Horatio Spafford and his wife, have endured the unthinkable experience of burying their own children.

BECAUSE THE BIBLE TELLS US SO

What allows these solid souls to keep singing? What empowers them to keep hoping, to keep believing, and to keep pressing forward in the face of gut-wrenching, heartbreaking, life-busting circumstances? What enables them to hang on to hope even as they limp through their suffering? It is the truth that they have discovered in Scripture, and it is the animating work of the Holy Spirit pressing this truth into their hearts and lives. God is who he says he is, a good Father who will never allow us to be separated from his love, and we know this because the Bible tells us so (Rom. 8:31–39).

Jesus is a faithful Savior and Friend, and he is making all things new in spite of the way things may seem. Things like death, mourning, crying, and pain, though they may seem to dominate the narrative, do not get to own the story line, and we know this because the Bible tells us so (Rev. 21:1–5). God's great and precious promises—that Christ has died, has risen, and will come again to heal the whole universe, that God so loved the *cosmos* that he gave his only begotten Son—these promises are trustworthy and true, and we know this because the Bible tells us so (John 3:16). When our lives are united to Christ through faith, we have the assurance that our best days are always ahead of us and never behind us, that every Christian's long-term "worst-case scenario" is resurrection and everlasting life, that our struggles represent a single paragraph in a single chapter in the middle of a story whose last chapter is a joy-filled, sorrow-free everlasting life, and we know this because the Bible tells us so.

What could be more irresistible than an inner resource that is ultimately indestructible? What could be more irresistible than a faith in which suffering and joy, sorrow and hope, rupture and rapture, can coexist? And how can this be? Because irresistible faith—faith *in Christ* to which Scripture testifies—promises an ultimate end to all sorrow and an everlasting continuation of joy, peace, and vigor for both body and soul. As the Heidelberg Catechism says in its own echo of the Scriptures themselves, our only hope in life and in death is:

> That I am not my own,
> > but belong with body and soul,
> > both in life and in death,
> > to my faithful Savior Jesus Christ.
> He has fully paid for all my sins
> > with his precious blood,
> > and has set me free
> > from all the power of the devil.

He also preserves me in such a way
    that without the will of my heavenly Father
    not a hair can fall from my head;
    indeed, all things must work together
    for my salvation.
Therefore, by his Holy Spirit
    he also assures me
    of eternal life
    and makes me heartily willing and ready
    from now on to live for him.[10]

Similarly, and as C. S. Lewis has said, at the end of time when Jesus makes all things new, "heaven, once attained, will work backwards and turn even that agony into a glory."[11] With the Bible as our reassuring anchor, we can know that all of our nightmares—both dreamed and living—will come untrue:

> Then I saw a new heaven and a new earth, for the first heaven and the first earth had passed away, and the sea was no more. And I saw the holy city, new Jerusalem, coming down out of heaven from God, prepared as a bride adorned for her husband. And I heard a loud voice from the throne saying, "Behold, the dwelling place of God is with man. He will dwell with them, and they will be his people, and God himself will be with them as their God. He will wipe away every tear from their eyes, and death shall be no more, neither shall there be mourning, nor crying, nor pain anymore, for the former things have passed away." (Rev. 21:1–4)

Knowing that our frail hearts would be tempted to disbelieve the reality of this future, knowing that our distracted and distressed minds would stray from this promise, Jesus took care to follow it up with the encouragement, "Write this down, for these words are trustworthy and true" (Rev. 21:5).

Indeed, there will come a day where sickness, sorrow, pain, and death will be felt and feared no more. These precious *Bible* words sealed in our hearts through the Holy Spirit are trustworthy and true. We are bound for the promised land. No matter our situation, our very best days are always ahead of us and never, ever behind us. How do we know this? Because the Bible tells us so.

So pick it up. Get into God's Word so God's Word can get into you. Read it, consume it, "eat" it again and again so the Holy Spirit can do his work in you. Keep at it until you earnestly say, along with Ezekiel and Edwards and Keller and John and Al and Spafford and Spurgeon and Lewis and all the others, that it all tastes like honey—even the hardest parts.

And when you do, in joy and in sorrow, it can also be well with your soul.

CHAPTER 3

SAVORING THE
PRECIOUS CHRIST

C. S. LEWIS FAMOUSLY SAID that when we read history, we find that those who did the most for the present world are also the ones who thought the most of the next.[1] In other words, the more heavenly minded we are—the more our heads and hearts are fixed on Jesus, his kingdom, and his purposes—the more "earthly good" we will be. And the more happy and healthy and whole we will be as well.

And yet, if we are being honest, we often struggle to keep our minds and hearts fixed on what Lewis calls the "next" world. With goals to chase, degrees to earn, careers to pursue, friendships to enjoy, families to raise, retirement accounts to build, and more, we are easily distracted from our chief purpose as human beings: "to glorify God and enjoy him forever."[2] Practically speaking, how many of us have the time and energy to do what it takes to be heavenly minded? Who has the bandwidth, the focus, or for that matter the incentive to "set [their] minds on things that are above, not on things that are on earth" (Col. 3:2)? Who has the ability to stop worrying about the details and concerns of the here and now and instead "seek first the kingdom of God" (Matt. 6:33)?

And yet, according to Scripture, the *only* way we can live full and fruitful and irresistible lives in the here and now—the *only* way our careers, families, friendships, and other pursuits can lead to healthy and life-giving outcomes—is to remain fixated on Jesus, his kingdom, and his purposes through each one of these pursuits.

Jesus must be the sun around which the solar systems of our lives find their orbit. He must be our single nonnegotiable, our "true north," and the wind beneath our wings. Otherwise, if we move Jesus to the periphery and center our lives on anything else, even our best and noblest earthly pursuits will backfire on us. When we turn good things into our ultimate things, they will go sour for us. When we plug our soul into any power source besides Jesus and expect it to give us life, it will steal life from us instead.

SWEET POISON FOR OUR SOULS

We each have something at the center of our souls that we treat as our functional treasure, as the ultimate source for our own happiness and significance and flourishing. Whether it's Jesus or someone, someplace, or something else, we all depend on *something* to save, sustain, and govern our lives as functional lord and savior. We tell ourselves, "If I can have *this*, then it will be well with my soul. If I can hold on to *this*, things will be okay. If my thoughts, words, and energy are centered on *this*, then my life will be worth living."

When we think this way, we become like the rich fool in Jesus' parable, who looks at all his money and material goods and preaches a mini-sermon to his own soul: "Soul, you have ample goods laid up for many years; relax, eat, drink, be merry." But God rebukes him, saying, "Fool! This night your soul is required of you, and the things you have prepared, whose will they be?" (Luke 12:13–21).

What makes this man a fool? First, he is shortsighted. With the mortality rate being one person per every one person, sooner or later he will die. When he does, he will not be able to take his things with him. They will offer no comfort, no support, and no salvation for him. As another rich yet much wiser man once said, "Naked I came from my mother's womb, and naked shall I return. The LORD gave, and the LORD has taken away; blessed be the name of the LORD" (Job 1:21).

He is also a fool for depending on created things to do for him what only his Creator can do. As Blaise Pascal once said, in each of us there is an "infinite abyss [that] can be filled only with an infinite and immutable object; in other words, by God himself."[3] Every pursuit of ultimate satisfaction outside of God himself will lead to *less* satisfaction.

In the Sermon on the Mount, Jesus addresses our tendency to replace Jesus with some other lesser and counterfeit "treasure" in this way:

> "Do not lay up for yourselves treasures on earth, where moth and rust destroy and where thieves break in and steal, but lay up for yourselves treasures in heaven, where neither moth nor rust destroys and where thieves do not break in and steal. For where your treasure is, there your heart will be also.
>
> "The eye is the lamp of the body. So, if your eye is healthy, your whole body will be full of light, but if your eye is bad, your whole body will be full of darkness." (Matt. 6:19–23)

Wherever we focus the "eyes" of our souls—wherever we *fixate*—matters immensely. If our souls look away from Jesus toward some other person, place, or thing to satisfy or govern or rescue us, every part of us will become unhealthy. Conversely, if our souls look toward Jesus, our relationships with other persons, places, and things will become healthier.

Few things illustrate the distortions that result from our unhealthy fixations better than J. R. R. Tolkien's character Gollum in the *Lord of the Rings*. Earlier in his life, Gollum is pictured as a happy little hobbit, enjoying leisure and laughter and friendship with his fellow hobbits. But all of that changes on the fateful day he gets hold of the One Ring—or, to say it more accurately, the day the One Ring gets hold of him. Gollum becomes so enamored with the Ring that he forsakes everything—his home, his friends, his safety, even his very life—in order to keep the Ring safe and secure in his own possession. The Ring draws him in, casts a spell on him, and occupies all of his attention and affections. It becomes his one true love, his *Precious*: "We wants it. We needs it," Gollum hisses. "Must have the Precious . . . So bright, so beautiful . . . Ahh. Precious."[4]

Tragically, this "Precious" that so captured Gollum's imagination and affection ends up stripping him of everything that is *truly* precious in his life. It also twists him bodily, ravaging him outwardly just as it does inwardly. And like a gulp of sweet-tasting poison, his Precious eventually ruins him.

The rich fool and Gollum are cautionary tales. When the eyes of our souls are unhealthy, when we fix our ultimate gaze on Jesus-substitutes instead of on Jesus himself, when we tell our souls, "If you can have and hold on to *this*, then it will be well with you," we set ourselves up for a fall. Once we start believing we cannot live without our own particular Precious—whatever it is—it is only a matter of time until we discover we actually can't live *with* it. We risk becoming useless—even counterproductive—for God's purposes in the world.

SHINING A LIGHT ON OUR PRECIOUS

Like Tolkien's Gollum, we all gravitate toward a Precious of some kind. We are, as the old hymn reminds us, "prone to wander . . . prone to leave the God [we] love."[5] And as a result we will begin, consciously or unconsciously, to hiss about our custom-made, personalized versions of the Ring, "We wants it. We needs it. Must have the Precious . . . So bright, so beautiful . . . Ahh. Precious."

According to Jesus, one of the most alluring versions of the Precious for us is money: "No one can serve two masters, for either he will hate the one and love the other, or he will be devoted to the one and despise the other. You cannot serve God and money" (Matt. 6:24). The Greek word Jesus uses for money is *mammon*, a word that encompasses both money and all the things money can buy. It's as if he is saying the best way to identify our version of the Precious is to simply look at our checkbooks and credit card statements, because wherever our money goes is where our worship is centered. Wherever we regularly spend the most amount of money with the least amount of effort reveals our truest, deepest loves. Where our treasure is, Jesus tells us, there our heart will be also (Matt. 6:21).

Another way to recognize what really captures our affections, what really governs our lives, what we really believe deep down will "save" us, is to look at where we invest our *mindshare*. Several questions can help us self-diagnose: What do I think about most? What preoccupies my imagination when I have nothing else competing for my attention? What keeps me awake in the late hours of the night? What causes me to worry the most? What worst-case scenarios do I tend to dwell on regularly? The answers to these questions often reveal what, or who, is most important to us, as well as what, or who, we are depending on to be our surrogate

Jesus. As Archbishop William Temple once said, our religion is defined by what we do with our solitude.

We can also look at what triggers our *anxieties*. For what am I willing to frantically tire myself out just to have it? What makes me most afraid of losing control? What, if I lost it, would rob me of a desire to face the day, or even to live? The answers to these questions also expose our true Precious.

In the same way our anxieties reveal our functional treasures, so does our *happiness*. What gives me the most contentment? What does or would cause me to express my loudest "Hip, hip, hooray"? What, if I were able to have it and keep it, would cause me to preach to my own soul, "Soul, you have stored up for yourself _____; relax, eat, drink, be merry"?

A final indicator of our true Precious is the nature of our *moral compromise*. What parts of the Bible am I most prone to avoid? Where, when Jesus or Moses or Paul or David or Peter speaks, am I most prone to look the other way, or to explain away what I have read? In what areas of my life am I most willing to say yes to sin and no to God and his Word? In what ways am I most prone to divert the eyes of my soul away from biblical truth and toward the way that seems right to me, but in the end leads to death (Prov. 14:12)?

EVERY "PRECIOUS" BESIDES JESUS WILL DISAPPOINT US

In John's gospel, we are introduced to a man named Nicodemus. Viewed from the outside, Nicodemus was a man who had it all. He was a ruler of the Jews (3:1), a religious leader (7:48–50), and a very wealthy man (19:39). In addition to all this, Nicodemus was a pillar of the community, with access to elite social circles and political power. By every measure, he was a portrait of success. But on the inside, he knew something was missing. In this way, Nicodemus is like football star Tom Brady who, in a *60 Minutes* interview at the peak of his success, posed a question:

> Why do I have three Super Bowl rings and still think there's something greater out there for me? I mean, maybe a lot of people would say, "Hey man, this is what it is." I reached my goal, my dream, my life. Me? I think: God, it's gotta be more than this. I mean this can't be all it's cracked up to be. I mean I've done it. I'm 27. And what else is there for me? . . . I wish I knew. I wish I knew. . . . I love playing football, and I love being quarterback for this team, but, at the same time, I think there's a lot of other parts about me that I'm trying to find.[6]

Sensing that something was still missing from his life, Nicodemus went to Jesus in the middle of the night searching for answers. Like Tom Brady, this man of great means was searching for meaning that no amount of success and that no earthly Precious could fully provide for him (John 3:1–21).

A second wealthy man from Scripture—we know him as "the rich young ruler"—approached Jesus on another occasion with a question: "Teacher, what good deed must I do to have eternal life?" For the rich young ruler as well as for Nicodemus and Tom Brady, accumulated wealth and status failed to provide the inner emotional and spiritual treasure that alone could bring him fulfillment and peace. With a hint of irony, Jesus answers the man's question by telling him that the only thing he can *do* to have eternal life is the impossible. He must obey the commands of God perfectly: don't murder, don't commit adultery, don't steal, don't bear false witness, honor your father and mother, love your neighbor as yourself, and so on. Blind to his own spiritual bankruptcy, the young man foolishly tells Jesus that he has kept all of these commands since he was a child. Yet in spite of such blind self-confidence, the man couldn't help but ask Jesus one final question: "What do I still lack?" (Matt. 19:16–22).

What do I still lack?

In Nicodemus and the rich ruler, we have two men who are supposedly living the dream. Both have acquired and secured virtually every Precious that the human heart would be prone to grasp: wealth, fame, pleasure, as well as some religion and moral virtue to top it all off. And yet, somehow, it just wasn't enough.

Have you reached all of your life goals like Tom Brady had at such a young age? Have you experienced unparalleled success and acclaim? Have you graduated at the top of your class, or made a lot of money in the market, or gained access to elite social circles, or gotten your body and mind into impeccable shape, or married the man or woman of your dreams, or raised children whom any parent would be proud of, or become a pillar of your community with immaculate religious virtue? If so, how's it working out for you? Have any of these things been enough to complete you, to give you the happiness your heart longs for, to enable you to say, "I've finally arrived!"? Or is there a nagging sense inside that you still lack something?

For many people, the pursuit of happiness is built on something that is not true, on a promise made by some Jesus-substitute or what Tim Keller has called a "counterfeit god."[7] And if you take away someone's counterfeit god, if you take away a person's functional lord and savior, if you take away a person's Precious—whether it be wealth, romance, career, physical health, friendship, or fame—you take away that person's functional source of meaning and joy.

The Nicodemus, rich young ruler, and Tom Brady stories tell us something else as well. While some lose their happiness by having their counterfeit gods taken *from* them, others lose their happiness by having their counterfeit gods given *to* them. When the things we possess become our Precious, it is no longer we who possess them; they come to possess us. And just like Nicodemus, the rich young ruler, and Tom Brady, when we finally get what we've always wanted, we come to discover it's actually not what we want at all.

The notion that our earthly measures of success and happiness don't always produce the result that we want is easily confirmed. Consider this list of men and women who grew weary of searching for answers to the question, "What do I still lack?": Nobel Prize–winning novelist Ernest Hemingway. Groundbreaking writer and literary patron Virginia Woolf. Celebrated and influential author David Foster Wallace. Seattle rock star Kurt Cobain. Oscar-winning actor Robin Williams. Pioneering poet Sylvia Plath. World-renowned fashion designer Alexander McQueen. Actress and cultural icon Marilyn Monroe.

All of these and many like them have two things in common. First, they all became portraits of success, popularity, fame, and fortune in their lifetimes. Second, they all experienced chronic misery from that place of success, popularity, fame, and fortune. Even in their great success, they were not able to find a Precious that could provide for them an ultimate happiness and peace.

Does this mean that success, popularity, fame, and fortune always lead to downfall and destruction? No, they do not. But they can still be tricky.

One of the most perplexing things that Jesus ever said was that it is harder for a rich man to enter the kingdom of heaven than it is for a camel to pass through the eye of a needle (Matt. 19:24). And yet, many affluent people in the Bible *did* enter the kingdom of heaven—Abraham the father of faith, Joseph the prime minister of Egypt, Job the wealthy sufferer, David the king of Israel, Solomon the son of David, Luke the physician, Joseph of Arimathea the financier, and (eventually) Nicodemus the wealthy pillar of his community—to name just a few.

Possessing what the world has to offer only becomes problematic when possessing what the world has to offer starts to possess you. Success in the world's eyes—wealth, fame, power, beauty, love and romance, comfort, popularity, health, and so on—can be something to celebrate and enjoy with thanksgiving . . . as long as we don't turn this kind of success into our life's lie, as long as we don't turn it into our Precious.

It's simple math, really. Everything minus Jesus equals nothing, and Jesus plus nothing equals everything. With Jesus, every other person, place, or thing we are given to enjoy is a bonus—not something to plug our emotional power source into, but rather something for which to offer thanks to God. As the poor cottage woman said as she broke a piece of bread and filled a glass with cold water, "What, all this, and Jesus Christ, too?"[8]

THE OLD HAS GONE, THE NEW HAS COME

To our fallen human tendency to grasp a Precious to replace Jesus as our functional lord and savior, C. S. Lewis wrote:

> It would seem that Our Lord finds our desires not too strong, but too weak. We are half-hearted creatures, fooling about with drink and sex and ambition when infinite joy is offered us, like an ignorant child who wants to go on making mud pies in a slum because he cannot imagine what is meant by the offer of a holiday at the sea. We are far too easily pleased.[9]

Explaining the biblical rationale that only Jesus can provide the ultimate answer to the question, "What do I still lack?" Lewis also said:

> God made us: invented us as a man invents an engine. A car is made to run on petrol, and it would not run properly on anything else. Now God designed the human machine to run on Himself. He Himself is the fuel our spirits were designed to burn, or the food our spirits were designed to feed on. There is no other. That is why it is just no good asking God to make us happy in our own way. . . . God cannot give us a happiness and peace apart from Himself, because it is not there.[10]

If Lewis is right, that God alone can provide the answer to the ache in our souls, then just how do we live in the reality that only God clearly lights our way? How do we store up treasures in heaven, while ceasing to store up treasures on earth? How do we seek first the kingdom of God and his righteousness, that all these things may be added to us also? How do we trade in our counterfeit gods for the one true and living God? How do we loosen our grip on the seductive Precious and then return the embrace of God, who alone can fill the "infinite abyss" that is our grand and glorious image-bearing souls?

The answer, from nineteenth-century minister Thomas Chalmers, is to be drawn in and overtaken by "the expulsive power of a new affection." For the spell over us to be broken and for our grip to be loosened, the counterfeit gods must be *expelled* and replaced in our hearts with the one, true, living God.

As the prophet Jonah warns us, "Those who pay regard to vain idols forsake their hope of steadfast love" (Jonah 2:8). Whatever Precious we believe will make us rich, in truth it will make us poor.

Whatever Precious we believe will make us strong, in truth it will make us weak. Whatever Precious we believe will make us happy, in truth it will make us sad. Whatever Precious we believe will set us free, in truth it will enslave us. Whatever Precious we believe will give us life to the full, in truth it will leave us empty. Whatever Precious we believe will satisfy our souls' thirst, in truth it will leave our souls desert-dry parched.

This is where it becomes painful, because this is where Jesus confronts our inner Gollum—that part of us that desperately wants to keep living in the dark, clinging to things that will wreck us if we look to them to save us. To the rich ruler, Jesus flips on the light switch and illuminates what the man is truly worshipping. "If you would be perfect," Jesus says to him, "go, sell what you possess and give to the poor, and you will have treasure in heaven; and come, follow me" (Matt. 19:21). Jesus is calling the rich ruler to release his desperate grip on his counterfeit god. Standing in the light, with his earthly treasures exposed, the man went away sorrowful, for he had great possessions. He couldn't let go of his Precious.

God have mercy on us if we consider any possession—whether it be wealth, fame, recognition, romance, career, or any other thing—to be so precious that we would choose *it* over *Him*. And we need this mercy, because we do keep plugging our emotional power cords into people, places, and things that will ultimately not breathe life into us but take life from us. We continue to cling to worthless idols and risk forfeiting the grace that could be ours in Christ.

To this vulnerability in us, this tendency to "wander . . . to leave the God [we] love," Jesus flips on the light switch for us too. As our hearts are illuminated, we respond by yielding all that we see to him—our money, our religion, our moral virtue, our acclaim, our friends and social networks, our kids and our spouse, and every other counterfeit god upon which we are leaning. We recognize that all these things belong on the periphery; only Jesus reigns at the center. He decides what your life will look like, how much power and influence you will have, what people think of you, what will come of your singleness or your marriage or your children or your friendships, what your net worth will be. Jesus says it's time to plug your emotional power cords into me, because I am your one true source for life (John 15:5). I am your shield and your very great reward (Gen. 15:1). I am your share, your portion, your inheritance, your true and lasting wealth (Num. 18:20). I am the one thing that you lack, the one thing you should ask for, the one thing your heart should seek, the one thing your eye should fixate upon (Ps. 27:4).

How far is Jesus asking us to go? How much is Jesus saying we must be ready to give up, to hand over to him, to ensure that our treasures will be stored not on earth but in heaven, where moth and rust cannot destroy, where thieves cannot break in and steal, and where success will never lead to catastrophe or despair (Matt. 6:19)? To this, he answers provocatively: "If anyone comes to me and does not *hate* his own father and mother and wife and children and brothers and sisters, yes, and even his own life, he cannot be my disciple. . . . So therefore, any one of you who does not renounce all that he has cannot be my disciple" (Luke 14:26, 33, emphasis added).

Could Jesus possibly mean this? The answer is yes and no. Here, he is using a literary device known as *hyperbole*, an obvious and intentional exaggeration in order to drive home a point. In light of his teachings about loving other people, including those who treat us like enemies (Matt. 5:44), of course he isn't saying a person should *actually* hate his family members. So then, what *is* his point here?

His point is this: Because Jesus has loved us so completely, because he sacrificed his life so he could have and hold us forever, because we *were* "the joy that was set before him" that made him willing to endure the cross (Heb. 12:1–2), because he treasures us as *his* share, *his* inheritance, and *his* wealth (Eph. 1:18–19)—we love him in return (1 John 4:19). For these reasons, our love for him should be so deep and so strong and so unrivaled that the love we have for our dearest people and even for our own lives should seem like hatred *in comparison to* our love for Jesus. For he, and he alone, is the true, hidden treasure worth selling everything we possess in order to buy the field in which he is buried. He, and he alone, is the valuable pearl worth selling everything we have in order to gain him (Matt. 13:44–46).

THE TRUE AND ONLY LIFE-GIVING "PRECIOUS"

There is something—someone—right and good to hold on to. Jesus is the true Precious who actually holds on to us. Instead of poisoning us, he gives us life. Instead of diminishing us, he makes us flourish. Instead of ensnaring us, he sets us free. It is Jesus who holds us and whom we hold above all else.

But if we do—if we go *all in* with Jesus—will we then end up neglecting, ignoring, or dismissing the significant people in our lives? Does gaining Jesus mean we will end up *losing* all the other meaningful people, places, and things we hold dear? Absolutely not! In a curious twist, it turns out that the key to *really* loving people well is to "hate" them in the hyperbolic sense of the word.

Think of it this way. If my love for Jesus is so strong that it leads me to "leave" my mother and father for his sake—if I begin looking to him to be my ultimate Precious to which all other loves in my life take a back seat—then my affection and loyalty to my parents will become *greater*, not lesser. This is true because honoring my mother and father is part of demonstrating my gratitude and loyalty *to Jesus*. To love Jesus is to obey his commandments, including the ones that say "Honor your father and your mother" (Ex. 20:12), and "Children, obey your parents in the Lord, for this is right" (Eph. 6:1). When my love and loyalty to Jesus exceed my love and loyalty to my mother and father, I will actually become a *better* son to them. You see, *in Jesus, I am more likely to become an "irresistible" son than I would be apart from him.*

Similarly, to the degree that Jesus is positioned above my wife and children in the hierarchy of my loves—to the degree that Jesus becomes more precious to me than they are—I become a more loving, more attentive, more selfless, more intentional husband and father. Why is this so? Because treating Jesus as my ultimate Precious includes loving my wife as Christ loved the church, cherishing her even to the point of laying down my life for her, treating her as my equal rather than as a rival or an inferior, doing nothing out of selfish ambition or vain conceit, but considering her wants and needs more important than my own (Eph. 5:25–30; Phil. 2:1–4). *In Jesus, I am more likely to become an "irresistible" husband than I would be apart from him.*

Loving my family well and rightly also includes being the kind of father who gives good gifts to his children, who raises them to love and obey the Lord, who instructs them in what is true and beautiful, who reminds them often how fiercely loved they are, who leads them without provoking them to anger . . . and who humbly apologizes and asks for their forgiveness when I fail to do any of the above (Matt. 7:11; Eph. 6:1–4; James 5:16). *In Jesus, I am more likely to become an "irresistible" father than I would be apart from him.*

When my inner Gollum is put to rest and my career takes a back seat to Jesus, I become an even better employee and boss. Why is this so? Because treating Jesus as my ultimate Precious includes doing all that I do, including my work, to the glory of God (1 Cor. 10:31). As an employee, I will seek to do my best work rather than careless and shoddy work—whether or not I am being watched—because it is ultimately the Lord I am serving. As a boss, I will pay a fair wage, I will not belittle or threaten those who work for me, and I will treat them with dignity and respect as my equals before God (Eph. 6:5–6; 1 Tim. 5:18). *In Jesus, I am more likely to become an "irresistible" employee and boss than I would be apart from him.*

Likewise, when money takes a back seat to Jesus, my relationship with it will become healthier and more life giving. Treating Jesus as my ultimate Precious and as my truest Treasure will lead me to give generously to God and to the poor and to people in need, to avoid debt, to save for the benefit of future generations, to pay the taxes I owe, and to provide for those who are depending on me for their care and their basic needs (Mal. 3:8–10; Prov. 14:31; 22:7; 13:22; Mark 12:17; Rom. 13:8; 1 Tim. 5:8). *In Jesus, I am more likely to become an "irresistible" citizen and neighbor than I would be apart from him.*

Lastly, being aware of how Jesus loved *me* even when I acted as his enemy will make me not only a better neighbor to my friends, but also a better neighbor to those who may regard me as their "enemy." Treating Jesus as my ultimate Precious will lead me to love not only those who think and believe as I do but also those who do not. It will lead me to serve not only those who like me but also those who don't. It will lead me to respond to insults with kindness, and to disagreement with understanding and empathy. It will, as Jesus commanded, lead me to love even those who are intent on not loving me in return (Matt. 5:44). *In Jesus, I am even more likely to become an "irresistible" enemy than I would be apart from him.*

When the love of Jesus captivates us, and when we begin to see him as the ultimate, true Precious, our hearts will have no choice but to love him first and to love him most. This will lead us to hold everything else loosely, no longer desperately tightening our grip. And yet, when we loosen our grip on these things, our loving Jesus sometimes has a way of giving them all back to us—and in an even greater, healthier measure than before. Just as the second half of Job's life was blessed twice as much as the first (Job 42:12), just as Paul the apostle found greater joy in a prison cell than he ever had as a violent yet successful mover and shaker (Phil. 3:8; 4:11–13), and just as the man who gave up all his possessions for a single, hidden treasure started leaping for joy (Matt. 13:44), so will our lives become rich when Jesus becomes our Treasure above all other treasures, our King above all other kings, and our Lord above all other lords.

As Jesus said, if we seek first his kingdom and his righteousness, all these things—the cares of this life—will be added to us as well. The way to gain our life is to lose it. The way to become full and rich in the truest sense is to pour out and generously give. The way to become the kind of person who does the most for the present world—the kind of person who has a faith that is irresistible—is to be anchored in the coming world.

We live inside the truth when we preach to our souls daily, saying, "Soul, Jesus lights the way for you. He has all of the resources you'll need for all eternity—all of your needs both big and small as he, your Creator, defines them. *All this and Jesus Christ too!* Rest now, soul. Enjoy, and be merry."

PART II

BELONGING TO AN IRRESISTIBLE COMMUNITY

A Christian fellowship lives and exists by the intercession of its members for one another, or it collapses. I can no longer condemn or hate a brother for whom I pray, no matter how much trouble he causes me. His face, that hitherto may have been strange and intolerable to me, is transformed in intercession into the countenance of a brother for whom Christ died, the face of a forgiven sinner.

—Dietrich Bonhoeffer

Let love be genuine. . . . Love one another with brotherly affection. Outdo one another in showing honor. . . . Contribute to the needs of the saints and seek to show hospitality. . . .

Rejoice with those who rejoice, weep with those who weep. Live in harmony with one another. Do not be haughty, but associate with the lowly.

—Paul the Apostle

CHAPTER 4

PRACTICING TRANSPARENCY AND KINDNESS

LIVING IN NASHVILLE, ALSO KNOWN as "Music City," can create some unique opportunities. For me, one of these opportunities is getting to serve about once a month as backstage chaplain to musicians at the historic Ryman Auditorium.

One evening, I met a successful artist who has several hit songs and travels worldwide, singing to sold-out, adoring crowds. In our conversation, I asked her what it was like being a performer—especially having reached the level of acclaim that she had. While having fortune and fame may seem glamorous, she admitted that relating to others chiefly through a microphone, screen, or written page can be painfully isolating.

With a pained look on her face, she told me that being a performer had become a source of sorrow. The frequency and pressure of life on the road had caused her marriage to crumble. She felt guilty for being away from her daughter as much as she was. She didn't have many friends because she no longer knew who she could trust. She could never know whether people wanted to be in her life because they loved her for who she was or because they wanted to use her for her money, her name recognition, the access she has to elite social circles, or the doors she could open up for them. Then she said, "In about five minutes I am going to walk out on that stage. Thousands of people's attention will be fixed on me, and they will sing along with all of my songs. Then tomorrow night I will do it again, and then again and again. You might think, 'What a life! She's living the dream!' But the truth is, being the person on the stage makes me feel like the loneliest person in the room."

In this vulnerable moment, she put into fresh words what God has been saying since the beginning of time: *It is not good to be alone.* No number of fans or sold-out shows will ever be able to substitute for our need to have friends. It is far better to be known and loved than it is to be followed, tweeted, and applauded. While not a bad thing in itself, this woman's celebrity had become an inadequate substitute for *actual* human intimacy and connection.

To the degree that it describes our lives, this lack of connection will render us unable to sustain an irresistible faith. Jesus said that the "one another" dynamic between his followers—that we love one another, pray for one another, speak the truth to one another, encourage one another and build each other up, bear one another's burdens, forgive one another as God has forgiven us in Christ, show hospitality to one another, and so on—is the chief factor of believability to the world with respect to our faith.

"By this all people will know that you are my disciples," Jesus said, "if you have love for one another" (John 13:35).

Lack of intimacy and connection and true "one anothering" also impacts us personally. Without this reality, our ability to sustain *any* kind of life-giving faith is neutered. We have been created in the image of a God who is both one and three. Simultaneously, he is the one true God *and* he is three Persons identified as Father, Son, and Spirit. As his image, being vitally and irresistibly connected to *him* requires that we nurture vital connection with others who are also connected to him. The curse of loneliness and isolation must be combatted—through the work we do on our own hearts as well as with each other—putting to use the resources that our one-in-three, three-in-one God has provided for us to do this. We need new patterns, practices, and postures that help us break the cycle passed down to us from Eden. Like Adam and Eve, we eclipse the "naked and unashamed," known and loved, exposed and not rejected state via our more guarded, community-killing patterns of covering ourselves, shifting blame, isolating, and hiding. New patterns will help us move toward knowing and being known, versus the shallower alternatives of *virtual* friends, follows, likes, and fans. For God has made us for community, not for isolation; for interdependence, not for autonomy; for relational warmth and receptivity, not for relational coldness and distance.

And yet, it will take much intentionality—both mutual and personal—for us to move in this direction, for my backstage friend's story is the story of us all. As with her, the surface appearance of our lives often presents a more connected, relationally full, emotionally satisfying picture than how things really are. Whether from a stage or behind a pulpit or through a screen, we look a lot more together than what we feel in our hearts. Our performances and profiles belie our reality. We, too, can feel alienated, isolated, and sometimes friendless. The curse that was first pronounced on Eve in the garden in Genesis 3—that relationships would be a struggle even under the best conditions—also touches our lives. Isolation can become painfully familiar to us, even at our own dinner tables. But what we must make sure of is that we never *settle* for that.

Here the observation of novelist Thomas Wolfe seems inarguable: that the central and inevitable fact of human existence is *loneliness*.[1] Whether we are introverts or extroverts, married or single, standing on the stage or sitting in the cheap seats, preaching sermons or listening to love songs, we all share the struggle to connect.

IT IS NOT GOOD TO BE ALONE

Why is loneliness a thing?

Why for so many of us does feeling lonely seem like the norm rather than the exception? According to the Bible, we experience loneliness not because there is something wrong with us but because there is something *right* with us. We experience loneliness because we know, deep down, that we were made for more connection, intimacy, and love than we seem to experience. We know that how things are is not how they are supposed to be. This is true experientially. It is also true theologically.

In the first chapters of Genesis, when God created the universe, he declared it all *very* good (Gen. 1:31). But God still saw something missing, one thing preventing his perfect world from being complete. "It is *not good*," God said, "that the man should be alone" (Gen. 2:18, emphasis added). It is striking that God declared this negative assessment in Paradise . . . *before* sin entered the world! God's perfect world still had one missing piece: Adam had no companions.

The answer God provided for Adam's loneliness in Paradise was Eve, a come-alongside companion, a helper corresponding to him (Gen. 2:18). Scripture reveals high regard and honor for those called "helpers." In fact, the other main character in Scripture who is given the name "helper" is God himself as he strengthens, protects, and provides for his people. God designed Adam and Eve together to share life and serve his purposes. "So God created man in his own image, in the image of God he created him; male and female he created them" (Gen. 1:27). When Eve is presented to Adam for the first time, Adam's artistic inclinations emerge, and history's first love poem is composed:

> "This at last is bone of my bones
> and flesh of my flesh;
> she shall be called Woman,
> because she was taken out of Man."
>
> Therefore a man shall leave his father and his mother and hold fast to his wife, and they shall become one flesh. And the man and his wife were both naked and were not ashamed. (Gen. 2:23–25)

A surface reading of these verses may tempt us to think that according to Scripture the sole answer to our loneliness problem is marriage and that those of us who aren't married are relationally incomplete. This reading is flawed for several reasons. First, as many with broken hearts know, sometimes the deepest forms of loneliness happen *inside* a marriage. This is especially true when a husband and wife isolate from each other and struggle to communicate, apologize, and forgive in times of discord. Marriage is not a "magic bullet" that cures the loneliness problem. Second, if it were true that only married people can be relationally complete, we would be forced to conclude that the Bible's foremost teachers on marriage—Jesus and the apostle Paul—were both incomplete.

But they weren't. Paul celebrated his life as a single man because it freed him to focus on kingdom concerns without distraction, even declaring that for those who are able, it is best to remain single (1 Cor. 7:8). Jesus, who was also unmarried, was complete from the beginning. He is "the image of the invisible God" and "the exact imprint of [God's] nature" (Col. 1:15; Heb. 1:3)—and none can be more complete than God.

Nevertheless, both Paul and Jesus recognized that it was not good for *them* to be alone, either. Each became deeply tethered to others, nurturing and enjoying an abundance of friends including both men and women. Paul took traveling companions with him virtually everywhere he went. In every town he visited, he developed deep, lasting friendships. Many of these he would mention by name and with great affection in his New Testament letters. As for Jesus, he had twelve intimate male companions—the disciples—including his most intimate circle of Peter, James, and John, plus several women including sisters Mary and Martha, and Mary Magdalene.

If Paul and Jesus needed friends, so do we.

Even in Paradise—and even if you are God—it is not good to be alone.

SOME HIDE FROM INTIMACY, WHILE OTHERS INVITE IT

When Adam and Eve rejected God's goodness and authority by eating the forbidden fruit, their eyes were opened, and they suddenly recognized that they were naked. This new, self-conscious reality set in motion a series of actions, each one a strategy to hide the shame they felt over what they had done. The more they hid themselves, the more distant they became from God and each other. Their nakedness, once a symbol of freedom, self-expression, and mutual enjoyment, suddenly became a symbol of shame. No longer feeling safe about being seen, they sewed together fig leaves to cover themselves.

To keep up the façade, Adam ran and hid from God. When God found him, Adam proceeded to make excuses and shift blame toward both God and Eve. To God, he said, "I was afraid when I heard *your* voice, so I hid."

Quite audaciously, Adam continued, "The woman *you* gave me, *she* presented me with the fruit, and so I ate it."

Eve also deflected responsibility, declaring that she ate the forbidden fruit because *the serpent* deceived her (Gen. 3:1–13).

This theme of deflecting, blaming, and hiding has remained with us since Eden. Painfully aware of our own nakedness and shame, we, too, have become masters at hiding from God, others, and even ourselves. Instead of fig leaves, we use other more sophisticated strategies to cover the things about ourselves that we don't want to acknowledge or be on the hook for. If anyone really gets to know us, if the real truth about us is exposed, surely no one—not even God—will love or desire us. If we let down our guards, we will surely be found out, abandoned, and forgotten.

As the story of Adam and Eve reveals, we have buried deep within us a strong tendency to hide. Interestingly, we also find in Scripture a very different strain. Instead of running and hiding and creating masks with which to cover their nakedness, the Bible's most exemplary saints *shed* their masks in favor of transparency and self-disclosure. Not only do they confess their sins, blemishes, and weaknesses privately to God, they also openly confess the worst things about themselves to each other and the world.

In the telling of his own story, Jonah reveals himself to be a grumpy, entitled, selfish, and hate-filled man (Jonah 1–4). Paul shares openly about his ongoing battle with coveting, bellowing out, "Wretched man that I am!" (Rom. 7:24). He also reflects on his prior life of being a blasphemer, persecutor, and violent man and concludes that he must be the worst sinner in the world (1 Tim. 1:12–17). Psalm 51, a beautiful and painfully transparent confession of sin, is introduced with the words, "A Psalm of David . . . after he had gone in to Bathsheba." In the psalm, David repents of his lust for Bathsheba and his adulterous sin in having intercourse with her while she was the wife of one of his most loyal soldiers and friends.

Jonah, Paul, and David were not seeking attention through melodramatic oversharing. Rather, they saw the value of sometimes putting their *worst* foot forward as a way to show a watching world how long, high, wide, and deep is the love of God. They wanted their readers, whoever they would be throughout the world and through the centuries, to become convinced that where sin abounds, the grace of God abounds even more (Rom. 5:20). In other words, they viewed the transfer of grace as something that happens not only between a people and God but also between people and people. It's a community affair, not a private affair.

Their confessions are a setup for celebrating grace and for reassuring people everywhere that if God's grace, mercy, and forgiveness can reach and transform the likes of them, they can also transform any kind of person. They wanted to convince the world that the one true God forgives not just once or twice but repeatedly, and that he forgives not just so-called little sins but also supremely shameful and significant ones. God, these ancient saints wanted the world to know, is above all gracious and compassionate, slow to anger, and abounding in love (Ps. 103:8). This is our irresistible God.

LEARNING FROM ZELIG

So why are *we* still afraid to go there? Why are we reluctant to reveal our true selves, even the less flattering parts? Why do we look at Jonah, Paul, and David and think, "Well, how wonderful for them—how wonderful that God would use *their* stories of sin, sorrow, and regret to demonstrate how far-reaching the love of God is," and yet still keep our own stories of sin and redemption a secret from everybody? Why do we still, even knowing how God can work through this kind of transparency, insist on doing everything we can to protect our brand, to manicure our profiles, and to never, ever let people think we are anything less than pretty and perfect and put together?

Why, when we know that God's smile shines on us permanently in Christ, do we still spend endless amounts of energy trying to control what other people think of us, thereby perpetuating the loneliness problem for ourselves and also for others? Furthermore, when we settle into patterns of hiding from each other, how can we ever expect to be transparent and loving toward our neighbors who do not know Christ?

Woody Allen's film *Zelig* helps us find answers to these questions. The main character is a deeply insecure, awkward, and shallow man named Leonard Zelig. Zelig is also described as "the human chameleon" because he routinely adjusts his personality to fit in with whatever group of people he happens to be with.

In one scene, Zelig is pictured as a compassionate servant of the poor, feeding the hungry alongside Mother Teresa. In a different scene, while in the company of Nazi soldiers, he raises his right hand and declares, "Heil Hitler!" At a party hosted by F. Scott Fitzgerald, Zelig hobnobs with the movers and shakers, awkwardly inserting himself into conversations and posing as an important, high-society sort. Soon after this, he is back in the kitchen with the servants and staff, hurling insults in a gruff, blue-collar-friendly voice toward all those snobbish "fat cats" on Fitzgerald's guest list.

Eventually, Zelig finds himself in a crisis because he realizes he has no identity of his own. His chameleon nature catches up with him. All those different personalities for all those different crowds of people, all those efforts to blend in, leave Zelig with zero sense of who he—*Leonard Zelig*—actually is as a human being. To address his problem, he hires a hypnotherapist named Eudora Fletcher, who puts him into a trance. The following conversation ensues:

> *Dr. Fletcher:* Tell me why you assume the characteristics of the person you are with.
> *Zelig:* It's safe.
> *Dr. Fletcher:* What do you mean, what do you mean, "safe."
> *Zelig:* Safe. To . . . to be like the others.
> *Dr. Fletcher:* You want to be safe?
> *Zelig:* I want to be liked.[2]

Zelig is a portrait of the human chameleon in all of us. Like the small reptile gifted with the ability to change the color of its skin to blend in with the environment, we often change our "colors" in different social situations to self-protect from those whom we perceive as potential predators.

Like Zelig, we want to be safe—we want to be liked—because rejection is simply too painful to bear. The chameleon in us—or what Brennan Manning calls "the Imposter"[3]—is represented by multiple "colors" or masks that we use to hide ourselves and fit in. We have a work self, an at-home self, an internet self, a party self, a church self, a bedroom self, and several other selves we depend on to keep us safe from exposure and attack. But this leads us to become disintegrated people versus people who are integrated and whole. In all our changing of colors to blend in, we become living pictures of the old comedic quip: "Those are my principles. And if you don't like them . . . well, I have others."[4]

It's safe . . . to be like the others.

We want to be liked.

This is what Pastor Jack Miller used to call an "approval suck."[5]

I'll admit it. I am an approval suck who is desperate to be liked. I am a human chameleon who is desperate to be safe. And so are you. But does the practice of changing our colors give us firmer footing, with more friends and deeper community and an irresistible quality to our faith? Or does it backfire and end up achieving the opposite, leaving us lonelier, more misunderstood, more ashamed, and more afraid? Yet even these tragic outcomes may feel more acceptable to us than the risks inherent in evicting our inner chameleon, because doing so makes us vulnerable. But avoiding vulnerability is an even greater risk, as C. S. Lewis observed in his warning about love:

> To love at all is to be vulnerable. Love anything and your heart will be wrung and possibly broken. If you want to make sure of keeping it intact you must give it to no one, not even an animal. Wrap it carefully round with hobbies and little luxuries; avoid all entanglements. Lock it up safe in the casket or coffin of your selfishness. But in that casket, safe, dark, motionless, airless, it will change. It will not be broken; it will become unbreakable, impenetrable, irredeemable. To love is to be vulnerable. . . . The only place outside Heaven where you can be perfectly safe from all the dangers and perturbations of love is Hell.[6]

In an ideal world, the truths of the gospel that moved Jonah, Paul, and David past the transparency hurdle should also provide us with the same ability. Because our sins have been forgiven, we truly have nothing left to hide. *If God is for us, who can be against us?* Because God has declared us to be blameless in his sight through the finished work of Jesus, we truly have nothing left to prove. *With us, our Father is well pleased!* Because God loves us dearly and nothing can ever separate us from his love, we truly have nothing to fear. *We are his treasure! We are our Beloved's, and our Beloved is ours!*

Even so, one remaining roadblock prevents us from entering into these realities and becoming free: *we are chronic amnesiacs.* Almost as quickly as we hear the good news that in Christ we have nothing left to hide, to prove, or to fear . . . we forget it. Because we are punctured by our own fallen condition, the good news of Jesus leaks out of us constantly. We need a better way to remember.

REVERSING THE NEGATIVE VERDICTS

I once saw a television interview with Mariah Carey, one of the most successful artists in the history of pop music, in which she said that if she hears a thousand words of praise and one word of criticism, that one criticism will eliminate the thousand praises in her mind.

Can you identify with this dilemma? I certainly can.

Praise and approval slip through our fingers like sand. Shaming and criticism, on the other hand, stick to us like Velcro and can feel impossible to shake off, no matter how hard we try. The serpent that tempted Adam and Eve, also known as the "accuser of the brethren" or Satan (Rev. 12:10), is the same deceiver of us—whispering constantly in our ears, "Did God actually say . . . ?" (Gen. 3:1). *Has God really said you are forgiven, blameless in his sight, and forever loved? Surely not! We both know you are guilty, shameful, and worthless!* The serpent hisses these lies to our hearts constantly.

This is why nineteenth-century minister Robert Murray M'Cheyne said that for every one look we take at ourselves, we should take ten looks at Christ.[7] Our chronic tendency to crank up the volume on the serpent's voice of accusation and bondage and to dial down the volume on the Father's voice of pardon and freedom makes this practice of taking ten looks at Christ into an essential, daily endeavor. If we are ever to move past our habitual, primal patterns of posing, self-defending, and hiding, then we must learn and embrace some new patterns of mind and heart. For this to be possible, we are going to need help from each other.

One practical way we can hear the Father's voice more clearly is to practice what Scripture calls "speaking the truth in love" (Eph. 4:15) with each other. We must, as writer Ann Voskamp once said in a talk she gave at our church, "only speak words that make souls stronger."[8] As the beloved, blood-bought daughters and sons of God, we must use our words to call out the best in each other versus punishing each other for the worst. To speak the truth in love is to offer encouragement, to put courage *into* a soul. One of our primary resources for doing so consists in the carefully chosen, life-giving words that God has already declared over us all.

If all of our Christian communities and churches were sold out to this one simple practice—*to only speak words that make souls stronger*—I wonder how many spiritually disengaged people would start wanting to engage. I wonder how many religious skeptics would want to start investigating Christianity instead of keeping their distance from its claims and its followers. Do you wonder the same?

It has been said that the best "outreach" we can offer is to *become* the kind of community that *we* would want to be part of and the kind of community that is difficult to find anywhere else. This might actually be Christians' best opportunity in the current cultural moment, where everyone seems to be on a hair trigger, always looking for something or someone to be offended by. I wonder if this simple, age-old, cost-free, compelling initiative is the key to turning a regular faith into an irresistible one. What if all it took for us to become the "light of the world" and the "salt of the earth" and the "city on a hill" to our friends, neighbors, and colleagues was to choose kindness over criticism toward one another, giving the benefit of the doubt over assuming the worst in one another, building each other up instead of tearing each other down. What kind of difference—if we committed ourselves to this—do you think it would make?

Do you remember that silly saying, "Sticks and stones may break my bones, but words can never hurt me"? I think Mariah Carey was a lot more honest than this in her interview when she admitted how much criticism stings. While sticks and stones may indeed break our bones, words can also wound us deeply and crush our spirits. Anyone who has received bad news, been shamed or criticized, or been the brunt of a mean joke or gossip understands this. Millions of men and women are in therapy because of wounds inflicted on them by *words* spoken to them either by others or by their own hearts.

Here are just few examples: *You are worthless. You are ugly. You will never amount to much. You disappoint me. Why can't you be more like your brother? You are too fat. You are too thin. I want a divorce. You should be ashamed of yourself. I hate you. I wish you were never born.*

However, words not only have the power to crush spirits; they also have a mighty power to lift spirits, to bring strength to the weary, to give hope to the hopeless, to put courage back in, to make souls stronger. Words like these: *You matter. You are the image of God. You are loved at your best, and you are loved at your worst. You are uniquely gifted. You are fearfully and wonderfully made. You are God's child, the bride of Jesus, the vessel of the Holy Spirit, and an heir of the kingdom. I see potential in you. I value you. I need you. I respect you. Will you forgive me? I forgive you. I like you. I love you.*

These are the kinds of words that lift a heart and bring healing to a soul. They can free the chameleon from hiding in fear and empower Leonard Zelig to discover and live from his true identity. These life-giving words can provide courage for the performer and poseur in each of us to come out of hiding, step into the light, and tell our true story—our blemishes, struggles, and sin, as well as the beauty, goodness, and mercy of God that we experience in the midst of them.

EVERYONE NEEDS THIS, INCLUDING PASTORS

To help our people turn down the volume on shame words and turn up the volume on words that make souls stronger, we at Christ Presbyterian Church nurture what we call a culture of *benediction,* a Latin term meaning "good word."

Every Monday, we begin our staff meetings by speaking life-giving words over each other. The purpose is to offer public encouragement, appreciation, and blessing. As expressions of God's relentless pursuit in each other's lives, we want to convey, "I see you, and I see God working in, around, through, and for you. I want you to know that you matter, that you are important here, that we are much better because you are part of us." We try to get very specific.

Angie and Suzanne, you are showing great leadership for all of us. Bob, you bring out the best in everyone else around you. Cameron, our guests are constantly telling us how hospitable and kind our church is—you are the inspiration behind this. Lynn, the music was lovely . . . again. Cammy, you are connecting our community to the poor, the marginalized, and those who are easily forgotten. Jesus must be so pleased with you. Mallory, God created you to love children. Jesus must be so pleased with you too. Scott, you kept your sermon under thirty minutes . . . we knew you could do it!

This benediction culture then works its way out to the congregation during our worship gatherings, especially as congregants surround the many tables throughout our sanctuary to receive the Lord's Supper each Sunday. As people approach the tables to receive the bread and cup, pastors and other leaders look them in the eye and speak life to them, in hopes of turning down the volume on their shame and guilt and sorrows and turning up the volume on their identity as daughters and sons of the Most High God: *The body and blood of Christ, given for you. Take, eat and drink, and be satisfied! In Christ, God has moved your judgment day from the future to the past. You are forgiven, blameless in his sight, and dearly loved! The last words spoken by Christ before his death, "It is finished," mean that the pressure is off! Now live in the light of how loved you are.*

Then, after being refreshed by the bread and the cup, our people connect with others around the sanctuary as they "pass the peace" of Christ to one another—offering prayers, confessions, greetings, and words of encouragement between men, women, youth, and children alike—speaking words that make souls stronger, putting courage back into each other's souls.

These benedictions extend far beyond staff meetings and worship gatherings. One time I was feeling like a failure because of a criticism I had received. The hardest thing about the criticism was that every bit of it was true. When I shared my discouragement with a friend, he responded by saying how proud he was of me, how he looked up to me as a leader, and how he sees God's hand upon me. Then he reminded me that the gospel I preach week after week to others is also true for me. Sometimes after a sermon, he will come up to me and say, "Hey, man. Nothing but net!" (We both share a love for basketball.) These kinds of interactions mean the world to me. They turn down the volume on shame and turn up the volume on grace. They put courage back into my soul.

As friends and family have preached the gospel in these and other ways to me, it has increased my courage to come out of hiding and renounce my inner chameleon. Instead, I am free to lean toward the ways of Jonah, Paul, and David and to consider how I, too, might view my story of rupture and rapture, of sin and redemption, as a means to help others see that if God's grace can reach me, it can reach anyone. As Jack Miller once said, God's grace flows downhill to the low places, not uphill to the pompous and put-together places.

And along the way, as we increasingly come out of hiding, maybe we will all become a little less lonely too.

Shall we go there? The health of our souls and the authenticity of our life together, as well as the "irresistibility factor" of our faith, depend on it. And whatever may come, Jesus will surely be in it with us.

CHAPTER 5

PERFORMING SOUL-
SURGERY ON ONE ANOTHER

I HAVE A CONFESSION: SOMETIMES my breath is offensive. What's worse, I often don't realize it. So to avoid being assaulted by my halitosis—and also to protect others—my wife, Patti, will tell me when it's time for a mint or a piece of gum. She tells me this not because she wants to hurt me but because she wants to help me. To ignore her would make me as foolish as a dog.

I say this as a dog lover. I am like most dog owners, who believe that their canines are loyal to the core, are always happy to see them, are reluctant to leave their side, and worship the ground they walk on. We don't want you to think we're the people we actually are; we want you to think we're the people our dogs think we are.[1] We get nothing but affection and admiration from our dogs—until it's time for the dog to have a bath.

Our Lulu is about as good as it gets when it comes to dogs. She is fiercely loyal, friendly to all, and house-trained. When you walk into the room, she greets you as if you are the most important person in the world. She simply couldn't be happier to see you. If you are sad or sick, she senses it, and will not leave your side until you are happy or well again. She truly *does* have the features of a best friend!

However, sometimes Lulu's breath is offensive, especially after she gets into the trash. Even worse, some days the stench of her entire body becomes unbearable—and she doesn't know it. When this happens, I do her (and the rest of us) the kindness of bathing her from head to paw. Lulu, however, does not receive this as a kindness at all, but as a vicious betrayal. Something about water and shampoo terrifies her. Anyone, she must think, who would subject her to this combination most certainly could *not* have her best interests in mind. As soon as the water starts running, Lulu swiftly abandons her role as this man's best friend. Instead, she turns against me and claws frantically at my skin while trying desperately to escape my grasp. Although she adores me in every other situation, when I try to help her with her loathsome stench, Lulu turns on me and treats me as an enemy.

AS DUMB AS DOGS

We human beings can be as dumb as dogs sometimes.

Imagine how foolish it would be if each time Patti alerted me that my breath was bad, I "clawed" at her by belching in her face and insisting she leave me alone. What if, instead of thanking her, I responded by asserting that my breath was not the real issue, but her nose was? What if I said to her, "Your sense of smell is the real problem here, so just get over it"?

When another person says they feel hurt by you, love demands that you don't brush them off. Instead, you must listen carefully to their concerns. Though there can be exceptions (when abuse is involved, for example), when someone else says that our words or behavior bring them pain, or that something about us makes life difficult for them and others, usually the most wise and loving thing to do is to take them seriously and humbly examine ourselves. This is true when our breath or our bodies are giving off an undesirable smell. Even more than this, it is true when a flaw in our character gives off a relational stench.

When this is the case, Jesus has provided us with clear instruction: "If your brother sins against you, go and tell him his fault, between you and him alone. If he listens to you, you have gained your brother. But if he does not listen, take one or two others along with you, that every charge may be established by the evidence of two or three witnesses. If he refuses to listen to them, tell it to the church" (Matt. 18:15–17).

Likewise, the apostle Paul wrote, "Brothers, if anyone is caught in any transgression, you who are spiritual should restore him in a spirit of gentleness. Keep watch on yourself, lest you too be tempted. Bear one another's burdens, and so fulfill the law of Christ" (Gal. 6:1–2).

King David, whose true friend Nathan confronted him privately for his sins of adultery and murder, also wrote, "Let a righteous man strike me—it is a kindness; let him rebuke me—it is oil for my head; let my head not refuse it" (Ps. 141:5).

Similarly, consider this confrontation from Scripture, as described by the apostle Paul. When Peter arrived at the church at Antioch, Paul publicly "opposed him to his face" for withdrawing relationally from Gentile Christians. The reason given for Peter's action, which Paul condemns as being out of step with the truth of the gospel, is that he feared the so-called circumcision party. This influential yet heretical group was advocating a version of Christianity in which the true insiders, those truly accepted and blessed by God, were those who not only believed in Christ but had also assimilated into Jewish culture by adopting Jewish practices, days, seasons, and extrabiblical laws. Paul's words to Peter were direct and forceful: "If you, though a Jew, live like a Gentile and not like a Jew, how can you force the Gentiles to live like Jews?" (Gal. 2:14).

Paul offered this strong public correction in hopes of steering Peter, and also others who had been drawn into his hypocrisy, back to a gospel sanity. Peter of all people knew that Christ's death on the cross, which removed dividing walls between a holy God and sinful human beings, also removes dividing walls between different people groups and cultures. In Christ, there is no male or female, slave or free, Jew or Greek—for in Christ Jesus, all are one (Gal. 3:28). For a leader in the church of Christ especially, excluding one group of people in order to stay in favor with another group is not merely a mistake; it is anti-Christian and anti-Christ. While Paul's resistance to Peter's behavior and the public nature of it may seem harsh, to preserve both the purity of the gospel *and* Peter's own integrity, Paul saw this gesture as completely necessary. In fact, it was the loving thing to do.

Even though we aren't given an account of Peter's immediate reaction to Paul's "resistance" toward him, we know that Peter had an appreciation for Paul's rebuke. And how do we know this? In a later letter, Peter refers to Paul's writings—*all* of them, including this part of Galatians that exposes Peter—as Scripture (2 Peter 3:16).

We also know that Paul's resistance to Peter's hypocrisy in Galatia would become foundational in helping Peter develop the courage necessary for the calling God had placed on his life as an ambassador (and eventual martyr) for Christ and his kingdom. Peter, who withdrew from Gentiles in Galatia for fear of what certain Jews might think, had also withdrawn from Jesus, denying him three times for fear of what certain strangers might think

(Matt. 26:69–75). But eventually, with the help and encouragement and redemptive critique from Paul and perhaps others, Peter would become one of the boldest, most courageous, and I daresay most *irresistible* preachers of the gospel the world has ever known. The fruit of Peter's courage, "inflicted" upon him by God in part through the faithful wounds of his friend Paul, can be seen in his biblical letters (both of which, in a beautiful twist of irony, inspire persecuted believers to have courage in the Lord) and in his bold evangelistic ministry in the book of Acts.

Stories of confrontation in the Bible, like that between Nathan and David, Paul and Peter, Jesus and his disciples, and so many others, can be quite challenging to me. I do not like being called out for *my* sins and *my* hypocrisy. In fact, I prefer to run from them. And every time I do, I miss an opportunity to become less like a devil and more like Christ.

No doubt, it is difficult for all of us to hear a word of correction, even from those who love us the most. But true friendship and healthy community cannot exist without it as a regular part of how we relate to each other. The path toward becoming the best versions of ourselves includes awkward and vulnerable moments that, when we submit to them, can have the effect of making us better for God and others. The cultivation of irresistible faith requires from us a level of humility that invites others to resist *us* whenever we get out of step with the gospel.

We value correction in virtually every part of life. Fathers and mothers spend thousands of dollars on counseling and books to help them parent their children well, with the expectation that they will need to *change* things about themselves in order for this to happen. Similarly, athletes stretch their bodies to the limit because a trainer tells them that a rigorous, gut-wrenching exercise routine is a must in order to compete well. Business executives adjust their leadership styles at the corrective urging of an executive coach.

Patients take medications that tire them, let needles penetrate their skin, endure rigorous physical therapy, and allow their bodies to be opened up by a scalpel because a medical expert has told them these things are crucial to their health.

A failure to give voice to difficult truths can be very costly. For example, if a doctor saw cancer on a pathology report but told the patient that everything was clear, the patient would die, and the doctor would be guilty of medical malpractice. Likewise, we can become guilty of *spiritual* malpractice by remaining silent about the destructive thoughts, words, and actions of the people in our lives. Recognizing this in his masterpiece about Christian community called *Life Together*, Dietrich Bonhoeffer wrote, "Nothing can be more cruel than the leniency which abandons others to their sin. Nothing can be more compassionate than the severe reprimand which calls another Christian in one's community back from the path of sin."[2] As the proverb says, "Better is an open rebuke than hidden love. Faithful are the wounds of a friend" (Prov. 27:5–6).

As a smelly dog needs a bath and as a sinful King David and apostle Peter needed correction, so do we need the truth spoken in love when we are giving off the stench of sin. Applying this principle to the friction that can sometimes arise in *true* Christian community, Dietrich Bonhoeffer wrote:

> Every human wish or dream that is injected into the Christian community is a hindrance to genuine community and must be banished if genuine community is to survive. He who loves his dream of a community more than the Christian community itself becomes a destroyer of the latter, even though his personal intentions may be ever so honest and earnest and sacrificial.[3]

WHEN "LOVE" BECOMES
CODEPENDENT ENABLING

One day when my family lived in New York City, I was in a hurry to get from one meeting to the next. The first step in getting there was descending from the twenty-eighth floor of the building where my first meeting took place. I was joined on the elevator by a mother and her young daughter, who smiled at me and said, "Watch this!" Then, with a mischievous look on her face, she proceeded to press every single button on the elevator wall.

Needless to say, I was late to my next meeting—thirty-five minutes late. But even worse than being late was that after the girl punched the buttons that would cause the elevator to stop at *every* floor on the way to the lobby, the mother said to me, "Isn't she just the cutest thing you've ever seen?"

Everything in me wanted to say, "Truthfully, ma'am, right now your daughter is the furthest thing from that." Instead, I held my tongue and offered a weak, disingenuous smile.

Several years later, I am still mystified by the mother's response to her daughter's act. Why didn't she stop the little girl from pushing all those buttons? Why didn't she treat it as an opportunity to teach her child about self-control, sensitivity to others, and the value of time?

Perhaps the mother passed up this opportunity to "resist" a bothersome behavior in her daughter for the same reason we resist similar opportunities: *we don't see them as opportunities.* Truth be told, most of us don't value confrontational truth-telling (or as Paul calls it in Eph. 4:15, "speaking the truth in love") because we are cowardly. The drive to be liked compels us not to rock the boat, even when rocking the boat has potential, if received humbly by the listener, to prevent the boat from sinking.

Even as I write this, I am reminded of how often I, too, have passed up an opportunity to lovingly resist hypocrisy when I observe it in those I am called to love. Sometimes I am tempted to leave a hard truth out of a sermon—even when it's right there in the biblical text—for fear of offending someone. Other times, if I hear a fellow Christian engaging in gossip, I won't shut down the gossip. Instead, I will listen passively as someone's reputation is attacked, or even participate in the attacking myself. Still other times, if I witness a fellow Christian speaking harshly to his children or to her husband, I will choose silence over the awkwardness of entering into the mess with redemptive correction.

Would a doctor do the same if she discovered a lump in the armpit of one of her patients? Surely not, because in the world of medicine, she would lose her license due to medical malpractice. Sometimes I wonder why we don't think similarly about our silence regarding patterns of sin and hypocrisy that we see in each other. Instead of calling it what it is—*spiritual malpractice* that allows a cancerous lump to fester within a human soul—we call it being nice. But sometimes being "nice" is the furthest thing from being Christian.

Perhaps this desire to be seen as "nice" is why so many Christians don't regularly tell others about the good news of the gospel. We have in our possession such good news of grace, truth, beauty, and everlasting Paradise offered to all who anchor their trust in the life, death, burial, and resurrection of Jesus. Do we refrain because we don't think it will be received as good news? Are we afraid it will offend someone and rock the boat? Consider, however, the following words from atheist illusionist and comedian Penn Jillette:

> I don't respect people who don't proselytize. I don't respect that
> at all. If you believe that there's a heaven and hell and people

could be going to hell or not getting eternal life or whatever, and you think that it's not really worth telling them this because it would make it socially awkward. . . . How much do you have to hate somebody to believe that everlasting life is possible and not tell them that?[4]

If an outspoken atheist would take issue with the lack of courage that prevents many Christians from speaking the truth about God and about life, how much more should those of us who *are* Christians take issue with the same—especially in ourselves? And yet, this isn't always the case.

THE CALL TO CONFRONT IS ALSO A CALL TO LOVE

While none of us wants to run around telling other people what's wrong with them, it is a mistake to think that *never* offering a critique—especially a humble one—is the most loving way to be a friend. In fact, sometimes love *requires* that we stand up and in humble boldness speak hard words to those whom we love. I believe this is what David and Paul both meant—at least in part—when they said that believers should be angry but sin not (Ps. 4:4; Eph. 4:26).

Anger toward sin in particular, though a negative emotion, should be motivated by positive love for those caught in it—similar to the reason a surgeon uses a scalpel on a patient with cancer. The surgeon will cut into the patient, not because she is against the patient, but because she is *for* him. Passionate for his restoration to health and longevity, she is against—even angry toward—the cancer that could cut his life short.

In a similar way, there is an appropriate and necessary anger that must be nurtured in our hearts toward the sin in others and in ourselves. As we channel our anger in this way—as we correct and rebuke one another, not as with a sword to destroy, but as with a scalpel to heal—we become channels of God's love toward one another. Love and anger go together. Both are necessary for the redemptive exchange that must take place between flawed sinners when one or both are "caught" in transgression (Gal. 6:1–2). Consider these words from Rebecca Manley Pippert:

> We tend to be taken aback by the thought that God could be angry. . . . We take pride in our tolerance of the excesses of others. So what is God's problem. . . . But love detests what destroys the beloved. Real love stands against the deception, the lie, the sin that destroys . . . "the more a father loves his son, the more he hates in him the drunkard, the liar, the traitor. . . ." Anger isn't the opposite of love. Hate is, and the final form of hate is indifference. . . . To be truly good one has to be outraged by evil.[5]

As a pastor, over the years I have had to preach hard words against the sin and foolishness to which we are all susceptible. As one who is called to preach the word of God "in season and out of season" (2 Tim. 4:2) and to use God-breathed Scripture to teach, reprove, correct, and train my flock in righteousness (2 Tim. 3:16–17), I realize that confronting sin is not an optional endeavor.

In my role as pastor—and also in my life as a Christian—over the years I have also had to arrange private meetings, and in some more serious and ongoing cases, group interventions, to challenge behaviors that dishonor God, that damage community, and that disorient those caught in transgression. These uncomfortable occasions have challenged sins like gossip, slander, divisiveness, aggression, sexual immorality, marital unfaithfulness, financial impropriety, greed, narcissism, and more. In some of these conversations, God has worked to bring about repentance in those I have confronted. In other conversations, the other person responded in kind—opening my eyes to things that I, too, have needed to repent. And sadly, other conversations have led to strained or even broken relationships.

I suppose what I'm trying to say here is that the "faithful wounds" God sometimes calls us to inflict on one another—always as with a scalpel and never as with a sword—can sometimes create further relational strain. And yet, because God's thoughts and ways are higher than ours, we must remain confident that God is at work. We also must remember that it is an unspeakable privilege to participate with God in one another's redemption stories, for "whoever brings back a sinner from his wandering will save his soul from death and will cover a multitude of sins" (James 5:20).

BUT AREN'T WE BEING HYPOCRITES HERE?

I know all of this, yet at times I have resisted this harder part of God's call and instead remained silent to avoid the potential discomfort and discord that truth-telling might bring. If I'm being honest, I have plenty of my own issues and feel hypocritical pointing out someone else's. What gives *me* the right to "go to my brother and show him his fault" or to "restore a brother who has been caught in transgression" as Jesus and Paul and James spoke about?

As a friend of mine and member of our church named Jeff Hays wrote in an essay on life and faith titled "I Love Beer and Jesus," inconsistencies in our lives can cause us to feel disqualified from challenging anyone else about anything. Jeff transparently writes:

I really like beer and drink too much of it. I yell at my kids way too much. I love beautiful women and admire them too closely and too often. I am crude, blunt and often times my sense of humor is only funny to me (and that is really all I care about anyway). I am a control freak, can blame and be critical. I am cynical, can be grumpy and, more often than not, people annoy me. . . . I constantly judge everyone I come in contact with— weird hair, ugly, geek, bad clothes, loud mouth, bad parent, and those are just a sample of the kind of things that have crossed my mind walking through the airport this morning.[6]

If all of us, like Jeff, have logs of hypocrisy lodged in our eyeballs, how can we see clearly to remove the speck from someone else's eye?

And yet, what person would *not* help remove a speck from someone else's eye? A speck in the eye is irritating and, if not addressed, can cause more severe things like infection and even blindness. For those of us with logs in our eyes, the solution is not to ignore the specks in the eyes of our sisters and brothers but rather to address the logs in our own eyes so we can see clearly to help deal with others' specks (Matt. 7:1–5).

Many times, I have felt overwhelmed by the logs in my own eyes. The week before one particular Easter, I disliked myself more than I had in twenty years. Here's what happened: At a dinner date with Patti, I opened up about my frustration with a certain individual and then tore the person to shreds in a gossip rampage. When I finished assassinating this person's character with my words, Patti looked at me and gently responded, "Scott, you know that you shouldn't have said any of that."

This faithful, corrective word from my wife sent me into a personal crisis. Anyone who listens to my preaching knows that I abhor gossip. I often equate gossip to "pornography of the mouth" because it seeks the same thing that a lustful fantasy seeks: a cheap thrill at another person's expense, while making zero effort to honestly connect with or commit to that person . . . in effect turning them into a thing to be used and a sick, emotional rush to get off on.

Patti's gentle rebuke got me thinking and took me to a sobering place. How can I presume to be a minister of the gospel and a communicator of God's truth? Having so easily cursed a fellow human being who bears the image of God, dare I use the same mouth to proclaim the blessings of God week after week? "With [the tongue] we bless our Lord and Father, and with it we curse people who are made in the likeness of God. From the same mouth come blessing and cursing. . . . These things ought not to be so" (James 3:9–10).

This incident jarred and alarmed me and sent me into self-loathing. It got so bad that I pulled Patti aside and asked her if she thought I was a fraud. Did she think it would be best if I just quit the ministry altogether? She was the one person in the world with a direct, daily glimpse into the darkness I was feeling.

The same woman who every now and then tells me I could use a mint didn't hesitate to agree that my heart is dark. But then she also affirmed my calling to pastoral ministry and the privilege God has given me—the same privilege he gave to the adulterous David, the murderous Paul, and the abrasive Peter—to serve as a spokesman for the pure and perfect One who is full of grace and truth and whose name is Holy. Patti told me that I do a good, consistent job of preaching both sides of the gospel *to others*—that (1) we are all busted-up, strung-out sinners who have no hope apart from the mercies of God, and that (2) God has met that need richly through the life, death, burial, and resurrection of Jesus. We are at the same time desperately in ruins and graciously redeemed.

"Scott," she said, "now is the time for you to preach the second part of the gospel to *yourself* in the same way you preach it to the rest of us week after week. Yeah, you are a mess. But the darkness in you can never outrun or outcompete the grace of God."

So, that Easter Sunday, I told our congregation that I had a theory about why my week had been as dark as it was. I think it was because God wanted to be sure that people who entered our sanctuary on Easter encountered a pastor with a limp. When we preachers limp into and out of our pulpits, God tends to do a lot of terrific things in the lives of our communities. But when we hop up there with a swagger, when we turn the pulpit into a pedestal or a stage instead of an altar, it's only a matter of time before our communities are weakened.

Anne Lamott once said in an interview that everyone is screwed up, broken, clingy, and scared, even the people who seem to have it more or less together.[7] That's just a wonderful way of saying that God's grace flows downhill to the low places, not uphill to the pompous and put-together places. As the hymn goes, all the fitness Jesus requires is that we feel our need of him.[8] Or as Tim Keller has said often, all we need is nothing; all we need is need. That Easter, these words became a fresh and sorely needed lifeline for me. When you're pretty certain that you are the most messed-up person in the room and you are the one with the microphone, that's a time when you need some serious reminding—both from Scripture and from the voices of loved ones and true friends—of how the grace and mercy of God hover over you and within you.

Like Peter, we are all duplicitous, sinful wrecks. We zealously confess him as "Lord," promising never to betray him, and yet within a few short hours we deny him like a traitor (Matt. 26:30–35, 69–75). But then he comes to us just as he did with Peter, reaffirming his love for us and also his intent to include us in his plan to renew the world and to shepherd and feed his sheep (John 21:15–19).

Consider this letter from a pastor to his son, sent to me by a church member after my Easter Sunday confession, from a time when his son was feeling useless as a servant of God:

Dear Son,

I continue to pray for you in the struggles you face. I've been so helped as I've thought about some of the following things. I don't want you to ever forget that Moses stuttered and David's armor didn't fit and John Mark was rejected by Paul and Hosea's wife was a prostitute and Amos' only training for being a prophet was as a fig tree pruner. Jeremiah struggled with depression and Gideon and Thomas doubted and Jonah ran from God. Abraham failed miserably in lying and so did his child and his grandchild. These are real people who had real failures and real struggles and real inadequacies and real inabilities, and God shook the earth with them. It is not so much from our strength that He draws, but from His invincible might. I am praying that He will give you courage in this quality of His.

I love you,

Dad[9]

So then, what qualifies you or me to steer anyone from a path of sin to a path of wholeness? It is certainly not having our acts together, for that would disqualify us all. Rather, it is in treating others as *fellow* sinners who are on a journey right alongside us. We move together *toward* perfection, being animated by God who is faithful to complete the work that he began in us (Phil. 1:6). In this posture, we are not adversaries of one another, but rather, we are what counselor and author Dan Allender has called "intimate allies."[10]

LEARNING TO RECEIVE

We are not only called to give constructive correction. We are also called to receive it. Just as our cowardice may prevent us from offering such correction, so our pride may prevent us from receiving it.

You might be asking yourself, "Wait a minute—isn't Scott contradicting himself right now? In the previous chapter, he emphasized how important it is to put courage into each other by speaking words that make souls stronger . . . to encourage one another and build each other up versus tearing each other down. Now it seems he is telling us that we must risk tearing each other down, and allow ourselves to be torn down, through mutual critique. Which is it?"

It is both. Encouraging words that build up *and* corrective words that steer away from sin and toward physical, emotional, and spiritual health are two essential sides of the same coin. When we honor both of these imperatives in our life together versus preferring one and rejecting the other, our community and friendship dynamics become healthier. But when we neglect either encouragement or correction in our life together, we invite unhealthy, distorted realities to rule.

As we consider the kind of friendship and community God wants for believers, we have to remember that true *Christian* community has a primary goal in mind—to present ourselves and one another to Jesus Christ as a lovely, sanctified bride "in splendor, without spot or wrinkle or any such thing, that she might be holy and without blemish" (Eph. 5:27). While this verse from Paul's letter to the Ephesians first applies to husbands and wives, it also applies to the Church—and to all friendship and community that claim to be centered around Jesus.

As Martin Luther stressed, we are saved by faith alone, but not by a faith that *is* alone. True faith will always be followed by growth in grace and virtue (Eph. 2:8–10). That is to say, while Jesus invites us to come as we are, he does not want us to *stay* as we are. Life in Christ has both a safety and a trajectory. The safety comes from knowing that Jesus, our faithful Savior, will never leave us or forsake us (Heb. 13:5) and that no one will ever be able to snatch us from our heavenly Father's fierce, loving grip (John 10:28–30). No matter how deep our regrets or how checkered our past, there will never cease to be a place of belonging for us in our Father's house. We are to God as the young, disabled Mephibosheth was to King David—who for Jonathan's sake would never cease to have a seat at his king's table (2 Sam. 9:13). For Jesus' sake, we likewise will never cease to have a seat at *the* King's table.

In this context of safety, there is also a trajectory that Jesus has established for us: we, his beloved daughters and sons, shall become like him, for we will see him as he is (1 John 3:2). In the end, and for our everlasting good, he will settle for nothing less. And he has given us each other so we can help one another along on the journey.

One view of friendship is nicely encapsulated by a statement typically attributed to Jim Morrison, lead singer for the Doors:

> Friends can help each other. A true friend is someone who lets you have total freedom to be yourself—and especially to feel. Or, not feel. Whatever you happen to be feeling at the moment is fine with them. That's what real love amounts to—letting a person be what he really is.[11]

This sounds good at first, and indeed it does highlight the importance of accepting one another and resisting the urge to judge one another for every little thing.

On the other hand, this sentiment can lead down some very tragic paths, as it ultimately did for him. Morrison, widely known for his self-destructive behavior, died alone in a bathtub at age twenty-seven. Who knows where his path would have led him had more people courageously and lovingly spoken up about his hedonistic lifestyle—the sexual escapades, the drugs, the nights upon end without sleep, the hard living—and had he the ears to hear the few people who *did* speak words of concern into his life.[12]

On the one hand, if we come at each other with all truth and no grace, we will become insufferable religious bullies—self-appointed moral police who constantly tear each other down and rarely build each other up. But on the other hand, if we go the way of Jim Morrison and give all grace and no truth to each other, we will become codependent enablers, preferring the destruction of a soul over an experience of social awkwardness.

But when we grant each other the Spirit-led blend of grace *and* truth, of love *and* law, of "Come as you are" *and* "I love you too much to let you stay as you are," we give one another the supreme gift of true friendship and community. Even more, we give each other a Spirit-filled, embodied experience of how Jesus would relate to us if he were with us in the flesh.

As the saying goes, "A good friend will always stab you in the front."[13] But the stab, when done in the way of Jesus, is done as with a scalpel aimed at healing, not as with a sword bent on destruction.

So the next time you sense a friend in need of spiritual care, take the scalpel and use it prayerfully and gently. And the next time a friend comes to you with a scalpel, don't resist it as if it were a sword—for your very life may depend on it.

"Faithful are the wounds of a friend, and profuse are the kisses of an enemy" (Prov. 27:6). The Great Physician—the One who uses only the scalpel on his children, and never the sword—himself has said so.

CHAPTER 6

EMBRACING HOPE INSIDE THE FAIRY TALE THAT'S TRUE

ON HER TWELFTH BIRTHDAY, OUR oldest daughter announced that she no longer believed in the so-called happily-ever-after stories.

"Now that I'm twelve," she said, "I know that all those stories are for little kids."

Apparently, our newly enlightened daughter had seen enough of the "real world" to conclude that *true* stories don't get wrapped up at the end with a nice, tidy bow. People fight and don't forgive, wars happen, couples get divorced, kids bully each other, poverty and oppression are everywhere, outrage dominates social media feeds, anxiety and depression are common, some illnesses can't be cured, tsunamis and hurricanes and termites happen, churches split, and everybody is going to die. "There is no such thing," she pontificated, "as a *real* happily-ever-after story. There is no such thing as a fairy tale that is *true*."

According to our twelve-going-on-thirty-year-old, the view of Shakespeare's Macbeth is truer than anything ever produced by Walt Disney or Pixar: "[Life] is a tale told by an idiot, full of sound and fury, signifying nothing."[1] As every thoughtful twelve-year-old knows, life is a wearying and difficult thing, and then you die.

Our daughter was by no means the first person to grow disillusioned about myths and fairy tales. C. S. Lewis, himself a master storyteller, grew up feeling a seemingly irreconcilable tension between his love for literature on the one hand and rational thinking on the other. While the romantic side of Lewis was drawn to happily-ever-after stories, his rational side would spoil the tales. While these stories functioned as a temporary escape from reality, to Lewis they were by no means reflections *of* reality.

This inner conflict between imagination and reason also led Lewis to reject the Christian faith he was exposed to in childhood. While stories like the parting of the Red Sea, the virgin birth, and Jesus' walking on water and rising from the dead amused him, they seemed far-fetched to his bright intellect. In many ways they did not square with science and reason, and therefore seemed false.

Then, in an evening conversation at Magdalen College with his friend and fellow writer J. R. R. Tolkien, C. S. Lewis experienced a transformation in his thinking. Tolkien explained how imagination and reason are deeply reconciled in the gospel accounts. In the words of British biographer Colin Duriez:

> Tolkien showed Lewis how the two sides [imagination and reason] could be reconciled in the Gospel narratives. The Gospels had all the qualities of great human storytelling. But they portrayed a true event—God the storyteller entered his own story, in the flesh, and brought a joyous conclusion [resurrection] from a tragic situation. Suddenly Lewis could see that the nourishment he had always received from great myths and fantasy

stories was a taste of that greatest, truest story—of the life, death, and resurrection of Christ.[2]

From that point forward, Lewis's perspective on the happily-ever-after story was transformed. Instead of being a mythical, untrue escape *from* reality, all the best stories became invitations *into* reality. Imagination and intellect were now reconciled as two sides of the same coin. The Jesus story for Lewis, as with Tolkien, had become the Story beneath all good stories, an alluring invitation—even for sophisticated and scholarly grown-ups—to look at everything with the imagination of a child (Matt. 18:3).

For a time, Lewis had found Christianity to be implausible, and on that basis resistible, due to intellectual and emotional hurdles he could not get past. But then an experience of community with his close friend Tolkien led Lewis to begin to doubt his doubts about God, truth, and the person and work of Jesus Christ.

After several months enduring a similar crisis of faith, pastor and philosopher Francis Schaeffer told his wife, Edith, that he had come to believe that there was one reason, and only one reason, to be a Christian: *because it's true.*[3]

NOT ALONE IN OUR DOUBTS

According to the Bible, our daughter, C. S. Lewis, and Francis Schaeffer were not alone in their doubts. Even the disciples of Jesus—those who had lived closely alongside him and seen him walk on water, turn water into wine, raise dead people to life, still a hurricane at sea, feed thousands of people with a small amount of bread and fish—would question the happily-ever-after story. Even though Jesus had told them ahead of time that on the third day he would rise from the dead, when resurrection actually happened they doubted. Perhaps they, too, thought such a happily-ever-after story was only for children:

> When they saw [Jesus] they worshiped him, but some doubted. (Matt. 28:17)

> Now Thomas . . . was not with them when Jesus came. So the other disciples told him, "We have seen the Lord." But he said to them, "Unless I see in his hands the mark of the nails, and place my finger into the mark of the nails, and place my hand into his side, I will never believe." (John 20:24–25)

When I read these words from Thomas, the nickname "Doubting Thomas" doesn't quite cut it. To me, it seems more accurate to refer to him as *Unbelieving* Thomas.

Yet there is an Unbelieving Thomas in all of us. Tales of such victory and resurrection are inspiring to the heart, but they can simultaneously seem far-fetched to the intellect. In fact, thoughtful people will be highly unlikely to accept a faith that seems dubious to them, no matter how inspiring its stories and affirmations might be. Such a faith will be easy to resist.

Deep down, we all need more than a faith that inspires us. We also need a faith in which we can be *confident*. We need to be able to say, along with Francis Schaeffer, that faith in Christ is not merely inspiring and intelligent and internally consistent—it is also *true*. And to be able to do this with honesty and integrity, we, like C. S. Lewis, sometimes need a person or community of people around us to help us remember not only what we believe but why. Otherwise, what would be the point of faith? Why would anyone want to nurture an "irresistible" faith if the faith itself is fraudulent?

Knowing our need for a faith anchored in reality, Jesus

provides evidence for his resurrection miracle—in the setting of community—to assure us he is alive and seated on a throne and that his happily-ever-after triumph is not merely a fairy tale. It is, as Christians believe, a faith based on real events that happened in time-space history. Therefore, it is a fairy tale that also happens to be *true*.

The Bible emphasizes this point. In Luke's gospel, for example, we are told that "Jesus *himself* stood among [his disciples] . . . they were startled and frightened . . . [Jesus] said to them, 'Why are you troubled, and why do *doubts* arise in your hearts?'" (Luke 24:36–38, emphasis added).

Here Jesus invites his disciples to doubt their doubts about his resurrection from the dead. Then he helps them by engaging their senses: "'*See* my hands and my feet, that it is I myself. *Touch* me, and *see*. For a spirit does not have flesh and bones as you *see* that I have.' And when he had said this, he *showed* them his hands and his feet" (Luke 24:39–40, emphasis added).

Based on such encounters with Jesus, Peter would later write, "We did not follow cleverly devised myths when we made known to you the power and coming of our Lord Jesus Christ, but we were *eyewitnesses* of his majesty" (2 Peter 1:16, emphasis added). Similarly, John would say, "That which was from the beginning, which we have *heard*, which we have *seen* with our eyes, which we looked upon and have *touched* with our hands, concerning the word of life—the life was made manifest, and we have *seen* it, and testify to it" (1 John 1:1–2, emphasis added).

The twelve disciples became so convinced of Jesus' resurrection that all but two of them (Judas and John) would later die as martyrs for the faith. As Lee Strobel writes:

> People will die for their religious beliefs if they sincerely believe they're true, but people won't die for their religious beliefs if

they know their beliefs are false. While most people can only have faith that their beliefs are true, the disciples were in a position to know without a doubt whether or not Jesus had risen from the dead. They claimed that they saw him, talked with him, and ate with him. If they weren't absolutely certain, they wouldn't have allowed themselves to be tortured to death for proclaiming that the resurrection had happened.[4]

In other words, the disciples were in the unique position of knowing whether they had truly encountered the risen Christ. If the disciples were purveyors of a conspiracy that they knew wasn't true, then they submitted to their own horrific deaths for a known lie. The more rational explanation is that they actually witnessed the resurrected Christ and staked their lives on this testimony.

The Gospels also cite how Mary Magdalene similarly and shockingly staked her life on her testimony of seeing Jesus risen from the dead. Mary, a former demoniac, was a first eyewitness of the resurrection. No one would have taken seriously the testimony of a woman like her. According to Jewish historian Josephus, a woman's testimony would not even have been admissible in a court of law "because of the levity and boldness of [her] sex." Celsus, a second-century critic of Christianity, mocked and discredited Mary Magdalene as "a hysterical female . . . deluded by . . . sorcery."[5]

If the gospel writers were merely trying to build a tight case for the appearance of Jesus after the resurrection, they would not have inserted the disreputable Mary Magdalene as the first eyewitness. There seems to be only one reason the gospel writers would have mentioned such a discredited source: because that is how it actually happened. And how wonderful that it *did* happen in this way! As was the case then, so it is now—that Jesus, time and time again, restores dignity and purpose to people whom society prefers to diminish, dismiss, and discard.

Another curious and otherwise unexplainable event is the conversion of Saul of Tarsus. As a highly educated, influential, and militant opponent of Christianity, Saul was stopped and blinded by the resurrected Jesus on his way to Damascus. From that point forward, he became Paul the apostle, herald of Jesus Christ and the resurrection (1 Cor. 15:12–19), and spiritual father to those he had once tried to destroy (Acts 9:1–19). There seems to be no other explanation for such a radical transformation besides an undeniable experience of the truth of Jesus' claims.

RESURRECTION (NOT) FOR DUMMIES

A thoughtful person might object, "Well, all you've done here is defend the Bible with the Bible. That is circular reasoning, which is unconvincing. Something more, something *outside* of the Bible, is needed to make a believable case for the resurrection."

I think that's a fair objection. In fact, I don't believe it is possible to *prove* that the gospel is true or that God exists or that Jesus rose from the dead any more than an atheist is able to *prove* beyond any doubt that these things are *not* true. There are many bright-minded, scholarly atheists who believe in the nonexistence of God as deeply as I believe in the existence of God. The likes of Stephen Hawking, Ayn Rand, Christopher Hitchens, Sam Harris, Jennifer Michael Hecht, Paul Kurtz, Peter Atkins, Patricia Churchland, and other thoughtful atheists come to mind.

And yet, just as there are many brilliant thinkers who do not believe in God and a virgin birth and the resurrection, history is also filled with people who followed a similar path as Thomas, the apostle Paul, C. S. Lewis, Francis Schaeffer, and scores of other thinkers and writers and scholars who came to the conclusion that God *does* exist and that Jesus Christ died, rose from the dead, and will one day return to inaugurate the new heaven and new earth about which the Bible speaks (Rev. 21:1–8).

In hopes of demonstrating that (1) our brains can (and should) be fully engaged not only in secular, academic endeavors but also in sacred, spiritual ones, that (2) the smartest people in the world include thoughtful Christians as well as thoughtful atheists and agnostics, and that (3) irresistible faith causes us to think more and not less, I offer the following additional thoughts:

First, as I have already mentioned in an earlier chapter, all of the Ivy League universities except one were founded by Christian ministers and/or laypeople. That's no small thing.

Second, it is also no small thing that C. S. Lewis was an Oxford scholar and atheist-turned-Christian who came to believe that "the heart of Christianity is a myth which is also a fact. The old myth of the Dying God, without ceasing to be a myth, comes down from the heaven of legend and imagination to the earth of history."[6]

Third, Dr. Simon Greenleaf, a founder of Harvard University School of Law, also came to believe in the historical, bodily resurrection of Jesus Christ. Greenleaf wrote the book *Treatise on the Law of Evidence*, which continues to be esteemed by many legal scholars as the greatest volume ever written on the use of empirical evidence to prove or disprove historical truth claims. Once an antagonist toward Christianity, the professor would mock the "resurrection myth" to his students. When challenged to prove his assertion by use of his formidable analytical skills, he accepted the task. But after doing his research, Greenleaf concluded that any honest cross-examination of the evidences for the resurrection of Christ would result in "an undoubting conviction of their integrity, ability, and truth."[7]

Fourth, Anne Rice, the brilliant and famed atheist writer of the Vampire Chronicles, wrote about her conversion to Christianity,

"The world of atheism was cracking apart for me. . . . I was losing my faith in the nonexistence of God."[8]

Fifth, there are many world-renowned scientists like Pascal, Copernicus, Galileo, Newton, and others who came to embrace the resurrection as true. You can add thinkers like Francis Collins, the esteemed architect of the genome project, and the many scientists and cutting-edge healthcare professionals in the church that I serve. All would tell you that their faith and their scientific knowledge, far from being contradictory or mutually exclusive, are deeply compatible with one another. Flexing their well-developed intellectual muscles, each would say that their faith supports and animates their science, and their science drives them to a place of awe for the God who created and sustains it all.

What's more, none of these scientists accept the secular claim that miracles are impossible, thus delegitimizing Jesus and the resurrection story. For them, it's quite simple. If there is a God powerful enough to create the entire universe, he is also powerful enough to suspend the laws of nature that he created. He does this to reveal his power, to provide assurance that we are not alone in the universe, and to demonstrate that our lives are infused with infinite meaning.

Based on these and the many instances of what the book of Acts refers to as "many proofs" that Jesus rose from the dead (Acts 1:3), it seems to me that it requires more faith *not* to believe in the resurrection than it does to believe.[9] In my experience, oftentimes people distance themselves from the claims of Christ for reasons that seem less intellectual and more emotional.

Recently, I spoke with a man who had heard the story of Jesus and the resurrection several times in his life. Yet this man seemed deeply defensive about, even overtly hostile to, the idea of becoming a Christian himself. I pointed out to my friend that he seemed not merely inclined to disagree with the gospel message but actually prone to attack it. I asked him why this was so.

After a quiet pause, he answered, "Okay, Scott, I'll tell you the truth. I'll tell you the real reason why I dislike Christianity. It's not because the evidence is unconvincing to me. In fact, the opposite is true. But I still don't ever want to become a Christian because if I do, Jesus will ask me to forgive my father for the ways that he hurt me."

I have had many similar conversations in which the person in front of me, when push came to shove, had few issues with the rational aspect of faith but used the rational arguments as a smoke screen. For each of these friends, beneath the surface was something about Christian discipleship—something about the narrow path of following Jesus in every area of life—that bothered them on a visceral level. For my friend with the difficult father story, it was a painful grudge he didn't want to release to God. The call of Christ, "As the Lord has forgiven you, so you also must forgive" (Col. 3:13), felt impossible for him. Others cannot envision surrendering to Jesus their approach to money, their sexuality, their prejudice, their addictions, their divisive and partisan attitudes, or their self-righteousness.

The resurrection and absolute lordship of Jesus Christ come as a package deal. If Jesus is risen from the dead, then it means we are accountable to *all* that Jesus said, namely, that we are sinners without hope apart from him, and that our lives belong completely to him. "Christ is risen!" means that he has a claim on our lives. He is the boss of us. He has full rights over us. He is Lord.

IF IT IS TRUE, THEN SO WHAT?

The next logical question becomes, "Even if the resurrection is true, why does it matter?" What difference does it make here and now? The answer to this question depends on what we think we ultimately need most.

According to the Bible, the greatest need of human beings is to know that they have been forgiven. One of the greatest inhibitors to flourishing is the shame we carry around with us. The self-loathing that arises from shame and regret can leave us in a state of emotional paralysis. Indeed, shame and regret can be a root cause of many emotional struggles.

Can you imagine a world in which more and more people began to believe, deep in their souls, that they are forgiven? This is the good news—that in Jesus, God has forgiven all shame and guilt from sins past, present, and future. If the resurrection accounts confirm anything for us, it is this life-giving and transformational truth.

Being forgiven in Christ serves as a central anchor and basis for Christian community. It is one of the things that makes *true* Christian community more irresistible than any other kind of community, because *true* Christian community starts with the truth that all of us are frail, broken, weak sinners whose only hope in life and in death is that we belong to our faithful Savior, Jesus Christ.[10] This kind of community is irresistible because, when its members begin to assume the characteristics of Christ himself, things like performing well and keeping our noses clean and keeping up appearances have *zero* impact on our acceptance in the community. When we come to understand that in the community of the resurrected Christ, the only basis for membership is that we are (a) messed up and (b) completely loved, forgiven, and covered in Christ, we become free to relate to one another on this same basis. Instead of rejecting and dismissing and retreating from one another due to each other's flaws, weaknesses, and sins, we forgive one another, just as God in Christ has forgiven us (Eph. 4:32). Rather than treating our differences as a basis for rejecting and dismissing each other, we move toward one another, learning to love across the lines of difference, even as Christ loves us. For in Christ, all who are weary are invited to come and find rest (Matt. 11:28–30).

Consider Mary Magdalene. Jesus' choice of this formerly demon-possessed woman as the first resurrection eyewitness was no mistake. It was an intentional, strategic gesture designed to bring Mary hope in the face of her wounded and sinful and guilt-stained past *and*, through her story, to bring hope also to us who, like her, are desperately seeking a place where we can belong.

Jesus, always intent on wooing us away from our demons and into his life-giving arms, does not come after us with a whip. Instead, he pursues us in the power of his resurrected love.

If you've ever read the encounter between Mary Magdalene and the angel of Jesus at the empty tomb, you may recall a remarkable mention of Jesus made in the exchange. In the gospel of Mark, the angel tells Mary and the other woman with her, "Go, tell [the] disciples *and Peter* that [Jesus] is going before you to Galilee. There you will see him, just as he told you" (Mark 16:7, emphasis added).

Those two words, "and Peter," are two of the most hopeful words ever spoken. When Jesus was going to the cross to die, *Peter* fell the hardest and betrayed Jesus the most. Not once, not twice, but three times Peter rejected Jesus publicly, denying with an oath that he ever knew him. Peter, the one who had once promised that though all the others may betray the Lord, he would not. But just as Jesus had predicted, before the rooster crowed, Peter denied the Lord three times (Luke 22:54–62).

In light of this painful betrayal, Jesus could have responded to Peter harshly. He could have invoked his own previous words to his disciples, that whoever denies him before men, he will also deny them before his Father in heaven (Matt. 10:33). But instead, to reassure Peter of his personal unchanging love, Jesus sends a former demoniac ahead of him to assure Peter that all is forgiven and all is well. No one is beyond the forgiveness and grace that Jesus offers and accomplishes with his own death and resurrection.

THE GOSPEL IS FOR HYPOCRITES, AND HYPOCRITES ONLY

One of the most encouraging things about the Bible is all the screw-ups who are mentioned whom God loves in spite of themselves. The "forgiven demoniac" and "forgiven coward" story does not begin with Mary Magdalene and Peter at the resurrection. Rather, that story traces back to the beginning where Adam and Eve, humanity's prototype and first parents, ate the forbidden fruit. When they did, the curse fell. Every person, place, and thing was suddenly busted up and broken down. Spiritually, socially, and culturally—humanity's prayers and worship, marriages and parenting, friendship and work—all of it became doomed to wreckage in the wake of that foolish decision of theirs, and of ours, to seek independence from our Maker.

But then, in comes the kindness of God with a blessing to reverse the curse. The seed of the woman (Jesus) would one day deliver a severe deathblow to the head of the serpent (Satan), and all would be right with the world again (Gen. 3:15). Resurrection and everlasting life. *Death in reverse.*[11] The world of suffering and sorrow and regret and curses and groaning passed away and everything was made new, because Jesus embraces the entire universe in his resurrected life (Rom. 8:18–25; Rev. 21:1–7).

After Adam and Eve, there came others. Noah got drunk (Gen. 9:21). Abraham offered his wife up to be abducted *twice* in order to protect his own hide (Gen. 12:10–20; 20:1–18). Jacob, whose name means "Deceiver," was a perpetual liar (Gen. 25:26); David committed adultery and murder (2 Sam. 11); Solomon was a womanizer and idolater (1 Kings 11:1–10); and Saul of Tarsus was an abusive bully and the chief of sinners (1 Tim. 1:12–17).

This is the community to which we have been called by God—a community that includes drunks and bad husbands and liars and killers and womanizers and idolaters and bullies. How does it make you feel to know this? It makes me feel hopeful . . . even irresistibly drawn to such community. Because if there is room in God's house for these, then there is also room in God's house for me.

The history of the Church has a similar story as these broken saints from Scripture. We see one flawed image-bearer after another, living contradictions of saint and sinner, lover and hater, good and evil, child of God and helpless wretch. As pastor and writer Andrew Wilson has noted:

> In many ways, the story of Christianity is full of light—mission, education, art, healthcare, abolition, compassion, justice. . . . But there is an undeniable dark side: attacking, burning, crusading, drowning, enslaving, flogging, ghettoizing, hunting, imprisoning, Jew-hating, killing, lynching, and so on through the entire alphabet. What makes this difficult to stomach is that the people involved, as far as we know, have loved God, followed Jesus, and received his Spirit.[12]

We could add to this that John Calvin participated in burning a man at the stake, Martin Luther made racist comments, George Whitefield owned slaves, John Wesley was an absentee husband, and more.

This "appalling history" presents another reason to dismiss Christianity altogether. The horrendous behavior of some Christians, whether historic or contemporary, can serve to delegitimize the entire movement. It has been said, "The only legitimate argument against Christianity is Christians."

But is this really true? Is the poor behavior of some Christians sufficient reason to excuse ourselves from considering Christ himself? Are the many failures, as offensive as they may be, enough to override and overrule an empty tomb? Will we lose respect for Mozart if a drunk man plays his music poorly at a dinner party?

As important as it is for Christians to represent Jesus well to a watching world, Christians' failure to do so is no good reason to dismiss the Man himself. As Tolstoy, a believer in Christ who failed miserably on many counts as a *follower* of Christ, once wrote to a skeptic friend:

> "You preach very well, but do you carry out what you preach?" This is the most natural of questions and one that is always asked of me; it is usually asked victoriously, as though it were a way of stopping my mouth. . . . And I answer that I do not preach, that I am not able to preach, although I passionately wish to. I can preach only through my actions, and my actions are vile. . . . And I answer that I am guilty, and vile, and worthy of contempt for my failure to carry them out. . . . I have failed to fulfill [Christian precepts] not because I did not wish to, but because I was unable to. Teach me how to escape from the net of temptations that surround me. . . . Attack *me* rather than the path I follow and which I point out to anyone who asks me where I think it lies. If I know the way home and am walking along it drunkenly, is it any less the right way because I am staggering from side to side! If it is not the right way, then show me another way.[13]

In the end, maybe it isn't the resurrection that presents the greatest scandal. Maybe the real scandal is that the family of God makes room for demon-possessed women like Mary Magdalene, cowardly betrayers like Peter, and Russian novelists who walk "drunkenly" along the path of Jesus. Maybe the real scandal of Christianity is Christians themselves.

A MANTRA THAT BRINGS HOPE
AND CREATES COMMUNITY

But what if the failure of Christians actually turns out to be the best argument *for* Christianity? What if the failure of Christians, in the end, is the thing that makes the Christian movement *irresistible* to billions of souls all over the world? The resurrection story represents the inauguration of a new world order, one in which a new community forms based not on how well God's people follow his ways but on how fully God forgives them of their failure and inability to do so.

Stories that tell of Jesus coming *first* to the likes of Mary Magdalene and Peter with the assurance of forgiveness, unfailing love, and life everlasting highlight his tender heart toward screw-ups. They are a taste of heaven brought down, signs and shadows of the world to come. They are also reminders that Jesus did not come to make bad people good or good people better, but to bring dead people to life.[14]

As my friend Ray Ortlund often says about his own place in the resurrection story, "I am a complete idiot, my future is incredibly bright, and anyone can get in on this." These words from Ray are referred to as the "Immanuel Mantra" by the church he pastors, Immanuel Church in Nashville, Tennessee.

Truly, we Christians can be idiots—we can utterly fail to seek, understand, and follow the life-giving ways of God. But what does

Ray's mantra say about our future—not just as individuals, but as a people? Furthermore, how does our future as a people gathered in Christ from every nation, tribe, and tongue (Rev. 7:9) impact the way we treat each other—with all our flaws and sorrows and sins—in the here and now?

First and foremost, the resurrection seals the fact that God has moved our judgment day from the future to the past. We who are in Christ are obligated to stop judging one another and instead get about the work of loving one another. We are called, now and to eternity, to live as what author Scot McKnight has called "a fellowship of differents," as reflected in this church's aspirational statement of purpose:

> In our life together . . . we will celebrate our diversity—opening our lives and hearts and homes to sinners and saints, doubters and believers, seekers and skeptics, prodigals and Pharisees, Presbyterians and non-Presbyterians, young and old, married and unmarried, leaders and followers, famous and infamous, our own races and other races, happy and depressed, helpers and those who need help, creative and corporate, conservative and liberal, American and international, affluent and bankrupt, public and private and home schooled—and all others who enter our doors. We will aspire to expand our "us"[15] by carefully listening to, learning from, and being shaped by one another's unique experiences and perspectives.[16]

Followers of Jesus *must* think about community this way, because the resurrected Jesus sends his disciples out to preach the gospel not only to our own tribe but to all nations, baptizing them in the name of the Father, Son, and Holy Spirt. We are called to invite others to a place of *belonging* in the global family of God.

Jesus welcomes all sinners, whatever our situation and whatever our past and whatever our regrets may be, to join him in the happily-ever-after Story that is true.

THE RESURRECTING OF ANN

One Sunday years ago at a church I served in as a pastor, a woman named Ann showed up. From the start, it was clear that her life had been shredded by hard living. Ann explained to our greeters that she was in recovery from a heroin addiction, to which the needle streaks and scars on her arms gave witness. She was barely thirty days sober. The people at the rehab center had encouraged her to "add religion" to her life, because religious involvement tends to decrease the odds of a relapse.

On her way into the worship service, Ann dropped her two boys off at the nursery. When she returned after the service, a woman named Jane broke some bad news to her. During the service, Ann's two boys had picked fights with several of the other children and broken several of the toys. Humbly, Jane said to Ann, "I'm so sorry to tell you all this, but I thought that as the boys' mother, you would want to know."

Impulsively, Ann responded by screaming an obscenity in front of a hundred or so children and parents.

What happened next caused my heart to sink. First, silence. Then an embarrassed, burning blush rising to Ann's face. Finally, Ann taking a "walk of shame" from the nursery and out the door, forlorn and beaten down—no doubt for the umpteenth time in her life—by the shame and regret and the familiar feeling of failure.

It would be easy for our church to recover from this nursery incident with Ann's boys. But would *Ann* recover? Could Ann recover from the shame that she carried out the door—the shame of a junkie-mom who took a risk, went to church, and screamed an obscenity in front of all the children? Probably not.

But Jane had an idea. What if she could reassure Ann in the same way that the angel of the risen Jesus reassured the demoniac Mary Magdalene and the coward-betrayer Peter? What if, roughly two thousand years after the fact, the resurrection story could be reenacted with life-giving, shame-reversing, community-forming words delivered, not by an angel, but this time by Jane, the nursery worker? What if, even in our own time, an irresistible faith could be put on display in such a way that it is not only shown to be *true* but also shown to *work* by bringing dead people, and their dead situations, back to life?

Jane sent a letter to Ann that read something like this:

Dear Ann,

It's me, Jane from the nursery at church on Sunday.

I'm writing first to let you know that all is well at church. No harm done! And the broken toys? No problem! We needed to replace so many of them anyway.

But what I really want to do, Ann, is thank you. Thank you for the way that you wore your heart on your sleeve on Sunday. That meant a lot to me, because I am often tempted to hide the messy things that agitate *my* heart. Thank you for being willing to be honest. Your courage to be honest got me thinking—what better place to be honest than church? You reminded me that Jesus invites us all to come to him raw and real—and to do that together and never alone.

I hope to see you again. More than this, I hope we can become friends.

Sincerely,

Jane

The next Sunday, Ann returned to church. Having limped out the door the previous Sunday, she returned with a spring in her step that said, "These are my people, and I want their God to be my God too."

And her people we became. And our God, the Resurrected One, became her God too. As her newfound faith grew over time, Ann would attest with a smile that she was a beautiful mess, a work in process toward her ultimate completion in Christ. Her presence in our community was so good for all of us.

And then, two years after cussing out loud in the nursery, Ann became the nursery director for the church.

There you go! A happily-ever-after story, right?

Yes and no.

Several years later, we received a call from the current pastor of that church. The message was short and heavy. Ann, having been many years sober, had relapsed, and she had died from a heroin overdose.

Ann reminds us that trusting in the resurrection is more than a mere intellectual endeavor. Without resurrection, there is no hope for Ann and there is no hope for us. If Christ is not risen, we are of all people the most to be pitied (1 Cor. 15:19). If Christ is not risen, we are still in our sins. And yet, Christ *is* risen. For Ann, this means that even though she went to sleep on a destructive high, she woke up in the arms of Jesus completely sober. Ann fell safe when she fell hard into the everlasting embrace of her resurrected Maker. From the first moment that she placed her trust in Jesus, Ann's judgment day was moved from the future to the past. Even at her lowest and most shameful, self-loathing moment, Ann was fully secure and loved. Jesus did not come to make bad people good or to make good people better, but to make dead people alive.

EVERY CHAPTER BETTER
THAN THE ONE BEFORE

For Mary Magdalene, Peter, Ann, and all who trust in the resurrected Jesus, what remains is a future with no more death, mourning, crying, or pain (Rev. 21:1–4). It is a world where we will be like Jesus because we will see him as he is (1 John 3:2).

After C. S. Lewis recognized Jesus in the Great Story behind every good story, he wrote a series of children's books called the Chronicles of Narnia. The final book in the series paints a beautiful and compelling picture of what is to come. Lewis imagines what it will be like for Christ's family of sinner-saints on the first day of the life that is to come, which we call the resurrected life. Referring to the lion Aslan, the Christ-figure in the series, Lewis reminds us that the highlight reel of even the very best earthbound stories will pale in comparison to our resurrected future. Take a deep breath, let your imagination be awakened by the words, and know that Jesus didn't come up from the dead only for Mary Magdalene and Peter. He also came up from the dead for you.

> As [the resurrected Aslan] spoke, He no longer looked at them like a lion; but the things that began to happen after that were so great and beautiful that I cannot write them. And for us this is the end of all the stories, and we can most truly say that they all lived happily-ever-after. But for them it was only the beginning of the real story. All their life in this world and all their adventures . . . had only been the cover and the title page: now at last they were beginning Chapter One of the Great Story which no one on earth has read: which goes on forever: in which every chapter is better than the one before.[17]

There it is. A happily-ever-after story that is also an echo of the ultimate, truest Happily-Ever-After Story. The myth that is also a fact. Words that are trustworthy and true . . . and by virtue of this, irresistible.

Let's remember for ourselves and go tell someone else this Story.

PART III

BECOMING AN
IRRESISTIBLE CHRISTIAN

*Movements that begin with the local congregation
in which the reality of the new creation is present,
known, and experienced, and from which men
and women will go into every sector of public life
to claim it for Christ . . . will only happen as and
when local congregations renounce an introverted
concern for their own life, and recognize that they
exist for the sake of those who are not members,
as a sign, instrument, and foretaste of God's
redeeming grace for the whole life of society.*

—LESSLIE NEWBIGIN

*"You are the salt of the earth, but if salt has
lost its taste, how shall its saltiness be restored?
It is no longer good for anything except to be
thrown out and trampled under people's feet."*

"You are the light of the world. A city set on a hill cannot be hidden. Nor do people light a lamp and put it under a basket, but on a stand, and it gives light to all in the house. In the same way, let your light shine before others, so that they may see your good works and give glory to your Father who is in heaven."

—JESUS CHRIST

CHAPTER 7

TREASURING THE POOR

FOR SOME, THE BIBLE IS a comfort. For others, it is a disruption.

Through the Bible, God heals with reassuring words of forgiveness, kindness, and welcome. Also through the Bible, God pierces with warnings meant to stir us toward repentance, restoration, and peace.

Jesus, the center of the biblical story, comforts the afflicted and afflicts the comfortable; he gives grace to the humble and opposes the proud; he is kind to shame-filled prostitutes and fierce with self-filled Pharisees; he gives special attention to the poor and denounces those who ignore the poor.

One of the most disturbing things Jesus ever said is that at the last judgment many will say to him, "Lord, Lord," and he will respond, "I never knew you; depart from me" (Matt. 7:21–23). He will also say the following:

"Depart from me, you cursed, into the eternal fire prepared for the devil and his angels. For I was hungry and you gave me no food, I was thirsty and you gave me no drink, I was a stranger and you did not welcome me, naked and you did not clothe me, sick and in prison and you did not visit me. . . . Truly, I say to you, as you did not do it to one of the least of these, you did not do it to me." (Matt. 25:41–45).

These words should jolt us, especially because they will be spoken to church folk—people who spent their lives attending church and reading their Bibles and giving their money and praying their prayers and getting their theology right and even preaching sermons and writing Christian books. And yet, like the ancient church at Laodicea, though they will have built reputations for being spiritually alive, Jesus will expose them as naked, poor, wretched, and blind (Rev. 3:14–22).

James, the half brother of Jesus and leader of the church at Jerusalem, linked genuine faith with an active concern for the poor. He wrote, "If a brother or sister is poorly clothed and lacking in daily food, and one of you says to them, 'Go in peace, be warmed and filled,' without giving them the things needed for the body, what good is that?" (James 2:15–16).

James answered his own question, saying, "So also faith by itself, if it does not have works, is dead" (James 2:17).

Earlier in his letter, James said, "Religion that is pure and undefiled before God the Father is this: to visit orphans and widows in their affliction, and to keep oneself unstained from the world" (James 1:27).

Both Jesus and James are putting a spotlight on our inclination to replace Jesus' call to deny ourselves, take up our crosses, and follow him. We replace his call with a self-serving path in which we deny our neighbors, take up our comforts, and follow our dreams. When we do this, we exchange true faith for a counterfeit. We exchange irresistible faith with a way of thinking, believing, and living that God himself will resist. Why is this so? Because demonstrating active concern for our neighbors—especially those whom

Jesus calls "the least of these"—is an inseparable aspect of a true, Godward faith.

The apostle John, who was probably Jesus' closest friend on earth, gave a similar warning: "If anyone has the world's goods and sees his brother in need, yet closes his heart against him, how does God's love abide in him? Little children, let us not love in word or talk but in deed and in truth" (1 John 3:17–18).

One of my predecessors at Christ Presbyterian Church, Dr. Charles McGowan, says that our doctrine—that is, our stated scriptural beliefs about God, ourselves, our neighbor, and the world—is the "skeleton" of our faith. Our doctrinal skeleton is a foundational, necessary structure around which the muscles, tendons, veins, and vital organs of faith must operate and grow. In other words, our doctrinal beliefs provide the foundation for our Scripture reading, listening to sound teaching, prayer, spiritual friendship, involvement in a local church, observance of the sacraments, and active love for our neighbors, including those most disadvantaged.

Yet as with the human body, so with faith: if the doctrinal skeleton is the *only* thing or even the main thing people can see when they look at our faith, it means either our faith is malnourished and sick, or it is dead.

Faith by itself, if it does not have works, is dead.

And a dead faith, like a dead corpse, is the furthest thing from irresistible.

WHAT'S YOUR MAJOR?

Imagine an exceptional college student. Now a senior at Harvard, she has achieved a perfect grade point average, is student body president, and is sure to become valedictorian of her class. She seems solidly poised to write her own ticket for graduate school, career, and life.

Brimming with self-confidence, the star student decides to nominate herself for a Pulitzer Prize for literature.

To her shock and dismay, the star student soon receives a short letter from the chair of the Pulitzer committee, which reads:

> Dear Star College Student,
>
> We regret to inform you that the Pulitzer Prize is a prize given to expert writers, not expert readers. Your application indicates that you have mastered the works of Charles Dickens, Jane Austen, Nathaniel Hawthorne, Virginia Woolf, and others. But until you join their company as a *writer*—that is to say, until you offer the world something, shall we say, "irresistible . . ." for the benefit of readers besides yourself—we must deny your application entirely.
>
> Sincerely,
> The Pulitzer Committee

A Pulitzer committee says to a literature major, "Excelling at reading literature does not make you a writer."

A lumberjack says to a boy, "Standing tall in a forest does not make you a tree."

A pilot says to a dreamer, "Flying from one place to the next does not make you a bird."

A doctor says to her patient, "Believing in your heart that the lump in your armpit is benign does not make you healthy."

And Jesus says to doctrinally sound, churchgoing, comfort-seeking religious folk who disregard the poor, "Doing 'church things' and being religious and reading your Bible every day and saying your prayers does not make you a disciple of Jesus."

James puts it vividly: "Even the demons believe [in God]—and shudder!" (James 2:19).

And with respect to ministering to the poor specifically, Jesus said, "As you did not do it to one of the least of these, you did not do it to me."

A TEST OF FAITH

Indeed, many build their lives on a foundation of religious behaviors and even sound doctrine, yet their lives lack an essential sign of God's transforming love in the heart—love for their neighbors, especially those Jesus called "the least of these" (Matt. 25:40).

But there is still hope. Even if we've been stuck in a doctrinally accurate yet relationally dead skeleton of faith, today can mark a new beginning for us. Why? Because God loves bringing dead bones to life with living flesh, and because his mercies are new every morning (Ezek. 37:1–14; Lam. 3:22–23). If salvation can come to the house of a formerly self-serving, greed-driven, poor-exploiting Zacchaeus, then salvation can come to our houses as well (Luke 19:1–10).

With Jesus, as long as we are breathing, there is opportunity for the Holy Spirit of God to breathe *his* mercy-loving, justice-seeking, salvation life into us. And when he does, neighbor-love and concern for the poor will begin flowing irresistibly through us.

Like a doctor catching cancer early and calling for surgery, or a father loudly warning his toddler to stop running in the direction of a busy street, warnings about our neglect of the poor are a kindness from God. His warnings provide us with fresh opportunities to consider how, as the hymn writer put it, "Christ has regarded [our] helpless estate and has shed his own blood for [our] soul," and how receiving mercy from Christ can transform us into participants in his mission of mercy to the hurting.

As Sri Lankan evangelist Daniel T. Niles has said, participating in Christ's mission is like one beggar telling another beggar where to get food.[1]

MAJORING IN THE THINGS OF JESUS

Living in the Spirit-filled awareness of Christ's love *toward us* will cause love to flow out from us toward others. "Majoring" in the things of Jesus will, over time, become more natural to us as the Spirit transforms us into his likeness. The "expert reader" in us will also want to become a "developing writer/participant" in the Lord's utmost concerns.

When this occurs, "We love because he first loved us" (1 John 4:19) becomes more than a pithy saying and vague aspiration. Instead, it becomes a very real description of our lives as we begin living out what it means to be redeemed, restored, forgiven, adopted into God's family, and welcomed to God's banquet table by grace.

In our own community in Nashville, this energy poured into the poor or "the least of these" shows up in countless wonderful ways. Some of our people invest their money, time, and skills to help those who've been released from prison find meaningful work and become law-abiding contributors to society. Others live and serve among people with disabilities and special needs. Some welcome orphans and foster kids into their homes, while others form support communities to wrap around them. Others partner and serve with local nonprofits that provide healthcare for refugees, post-trauma resources for women coming out of prostitution, healing community for those caught in addiction, care and support for those facing a crisis pregnancy, and counseling, resourcing, and friendship for those suffering divorce or bereavement or unemployment or loneliness or anxiety or depression. And there is so much more!

Our church is by no means the only community of Christians who turn their hearts and lives toward the least of these as a way of life. In fact, millions of Christians worldwide are doing the same every single day. The mercy and justice impulse among God's people is so strong that Nicholas Kristof of the *New York Times*, a skeptic, has written at length about it. Based on his personal observations while covering disasters and poverty all over the world, Kristof wrote:

> In reporting on poverty, disease and oppression . . . [Christians] are disproportionately likely to donate 10 percent of their incomes to charities . . . more important, go to the front lines, at home or abroad, in the battles against hunger, malaria, prison rape, obstetric fistula, human trafficking or genocide, and some of the bravest people you meet are . . . Christians. . . . *I'm not particularly religious myself,* but I stand in awe of those I've seen risking their lives in this way—and it sickens me to see that faith mocked at New York cocktail parties.[2]

The reason Christians all over the world invest their lives so sacrificially is simple: they have come to believe that God's gifts and graces are never meant to be hoarded but always meant to be shared. An overflowing cup (Ps. 23:5) will spill over into the lives of others.

Whether we have little or plenty, life in Christ *plus nothing else* makes us the wealthiest people in the world. We who are in Christ are *rich* in his saving grace, *rich* in the status he has given us as beloved daughters and sons, *rich* in assurance that nothing in all creation will ever be able to separate us from his love, *rich* in the knowledge that he has plans to prosper us and not to harm us—and in light of all this, we are called to be *rich* in the overflow of love and good deeds (2 Cor. 8:9; Gal. 3:29; Titus 3:5; Rom. 8:38–39; Jer. 29:11–13; Heb. 10:24).

As we in our church community often remind ourselves and each other—and as I've noted earlier—the gospel boils down to basic math:

Everything minus Jesus equals nothing.
Jesus plus nothing equals everything.

And if these equations are true, then we have nothing to lose when we give ourselves away and everything to gain. In the end, the greatest beneficiaries—even more than the ones who do the receiving—are the ones who do the giving. We lose our lives when we try to hold on to them, and we gain our lives when we lay them down in love and service to God and neighbor (Luke 9:24).

Where there is true faith, the vital signs will always show up. When the Spirit of Christ inhabits us, more will be visible than a mere doctrinal skeleton. In the same way that pulse and breath indicate life in the body, love and good deeds and generosity toward the poor indicate life in the soul and life in our communities of faith.

Even though he is the creator of words and the architect of human biology, Jesus did not major in literature or medicine. In fact, he didn't attend any higher institutions of learning because his parents, Joseph and Mary, couldn't afford to send him. But Jesus *did* have a mission, he *did* have a driving passion, and he *did* have an agenda around which he organized his thoughts, words, actions, and life trajectory.

Here is how Jesus unveiled his public ministry and message:

[Jesus] went to the synagogue on the Sabbath day, and he stood up to read. And the scroll of the prophet Isaiah was given to him. He unrolled the scroll and found the place where it was written,

> "The Spirit of the Lord is upon me,
>> because he has anointed me
>> to proclaim good news to the poor.
> He has sent me to proclaim liberty to the captives
>> and recovering of sight to the blind,
>> to set at liberty those who are oppressed,
>> to proclaim the year of the Lord's favor."

And he rolled up the scroll and gave it back to the attendant and sat down. And the eyes of all in the synagogue were fixed on him. And he began to say to them, "Today this Scripture has been fulfilled in your hearing." (Luke 4:16–21)

What's more, when Jesus envisioned a banquet, here is the guest list he imagined:

"Quickly, get out into the city streets and alleys. Collect all who look like they need a square meal, all the misfits and homeless and wretched you can lay your hands on, and bring them here. . . . Then go to the country roads. Whoever you find, drag them in. I want my house full!" (Luke 14:21–24 MSG)

Jesus' zeal to give special attention to "all the misfits and homeless and wretched" is an echo of what had been said long before to the people of God through Moses:

"There will be no poor among you. . . . If among you, one of your brothers should become poor . . . you shall not harden your heart or shut your hand against your poor brother, but you shall open your hand to him and lend him sufficient for his need, whatever it may be. . . . You shall give to him freely, and your heart shall not be grudging when you give to him. . . . You shall not let him go empty-handed. . . . As the LORD your God has blessed you, you shall give to him." (Deut. 15:4, 7–8, 10, 13–14)

Why else would David look at Mephibosheth, the orphaned son of Jonathan who was crippled in both feet, and offer reassurance that he possessed the status of a royal son and that there would always be a seat for him at the king's table (2 Sam. 9:13)? David was doing what is only natural for the supernaturally redeemed, restored, forgiven, "mercied" daughters and sons of God. As a sinner saved by grace, having discovered through experience that all the fitness God required of him was to feel his need of God, David became compelled by mercy—not only as a recipient but also as a generous giver of it.

David discovered, as millions of others also have, that it is more blessed—that is, it is *happier* and *healthier*—to give than it is to receive (Acts 20:35). Our enjoyment of God's gifts, including his mercy and compassion toward us, is made complete only when we've spent our lives sharing them with others in the human community.

Giving special attention to the poor also became second nature to the priorities, culture, and mission of the New Testament church. These first Christians knew Jesus as the self-donating Prince of Peace who became poor, entered the world via a borrowed barn, became a child refugee, was raised in a small and disregarded town, had no place to lay his head, was in his appearance more homely than handsome (Isa. 53:2), and left the world as a despised, rejected, shamed, falsely accused, crucified criminal. These early Christians were so enthralled with the Jesus they knew that they found joy in imitating him. Rather than hoarding God's kindness, they became openhanded with earth's treasures for the good of their neighbors—especially those who were wrecked, weary, and accustomed to scarcity.

These first Christians shared their homes, their tables, their time, and their material wealth liberally, in such a way that no one claimed his possessions were his own. They were generous with all they had, even selling lands and homes, if necessary, to ensure that there were no needy people among them. Their generosity was so profound and so public that they had "favor with all the people"— including their nonbelieving neighbors (Acts 2:47; 4:32–37).

Likewise, the apostle Paul spoke of how *eager* he and his companions were to remember the poor, as the churches who supported them were also *eager* for them to do (Gal. 2:10). And sometimes those who are most eager to bless others with an irresistible generosity are God's faithful who themselves possess very little. There is the poor widow, for instance, who gave her last coin in the temple as an expression of gratitude for the riches she had received in Christ (Luke 21:1–4). There were also the Macedonians who, though they were economically strapped—experiencing the equivalent of a deep and prolonged recession—nonetheless emptied their pockets and purses to help finance the spread of the gospel and relief to the Lord's poor through Paul:

> We want you to know, brothers, about the grace of God that has been given among the churches of Macedonia, for in a severe test of affliction, their abundance of joy and their extreme poverty have overflowed in a wealth of generosity on their part. For they gave according to their means, as I can testify, and beyond their means, of their own accord, *begging us earnestly*

for the favor of taking part in the relief of the saints—and this, not as we expected, but they gave themselves first to the Lord and then by the will of God to us. (2 Cor. 8:1–5, emphasis added)

Did you catch that? The Macedonians, who had fallen on hard times themselves, begged Paul and the other apostles for an opportunity to help provide relief for others who, like them, were suffering from economic scarcity. Sometimes the people with the most generous hearts are those who themselves live in scarcity, perhaps because in their scarcity, they are more sensitive to the reality that all of life is a gift from God, and that Jesus plus nothing equals everything.

Not long ago, a husband and wife in our church fell on hard times financially. For the purposes of being known and receiving prayer, they quietly confided in a church leader about their situation. Not long after this, the leader and the couple were at a small gathering of church members together. At the gathering, the leader took it upon herself to announce that an "anonymous couple from our church" were struggling financially. If anyone wanted to make a contribution to assist them—maybe twenty-five or fifty dollars each—she would gladly collect the gifts and deliver the total to the anonymous couple the next day.

Desiring to help those less fortunate, several people handed cash and checks to the leader. The next morning, as she added up the gifts, she discovered one check made out for an amount that was substantially larger than the others. This generous check— given to alleviate the burden of the "anonymous couple"—had been donated by the anonymous couple themselves. Not having any idea that they were donating for the purpose of alleviating their *own* burden, they gave out of their own scarcity.

HOW COMFORT, CONTROL, AND
FEAR CAN HOLD US BACK

So why doesn't every Christian community today mirror the actions and attitudes of this couple in financial straits, or of the widow who gave her mite, or of the Macedonians who *begged* for opportunities to contribute to others in need? What factors hold us back from a faith that is irresistible because of the unexplainable, eager generosity—especially toward those who live in scarcity—to which it leads? I believe there are a handful of factors.

First, the idea of laboring to help improve conditions for the poor can seem overwhelming. Even Jesus said that the poor will always be with us, no matter how hard we try to end the suffering (Mark 14:7). With hundreds of millions of people around the world living in extreme poverty, what difference can even our best efforts truly make? If national governments can't solve the problem of poverty, how on earth can we?

Second, getting involved with the poor can include exposing ourselves to the messiness of things like homelessness, disease, addiction, and mental illness. Scripture's clear and comprehensive call to "do justice and to love kindness" (Micah 6:8) sounds inspiring from the safe, controlled confines of our private lives and air-conditioned worship services and personal quiet times. But every step toward *doing* justice and *loving* kindness requires a step away from the safe, controlled way of life upon which we have learned to depend. It calls us to lay down our lives. It beckons us to start taking up our crosses daily and *following* Jesus into the very places we would likely find him if he were still with us in the flesh.

We are reluctant to let ourselves be awakened to the fact that suffering is everywhere and that it is *our* calling to be the hands and feet of Christ and address it. How hard it is to face reality:

that in some places life expectancy is a mere fifty years[3] and infant mortality is as high as 10 percent,[4] that there are between 20 and 30 million human trafficking victims worldwide,[5] that 75 percent of US women in a crisis pregnancy are from low-income or poor situations,[6] that most children will never have a chance to attend college, and that even people living two doors down are fighting hard, hidden battles with loneliness, addiction, mental illness, guilt, shame, regret, and hopelessness. We can feel paralyzed and unsure how to take steps toward "majoring" in the kind of neighbor-love that Jesus demonstrated. When it comes down to it, we feel ill equipped, unsure of ourselves, and scared of making things worse instead of better.

Third, some of us nurse a dismissive attitude toward the poor based on blind and self-righteous partisan politics, or even worse, a false belief that poverty is mainly the fault of the poor themselves. In the same way the disciples assumed the condition of blindness was *necessarily* because of the sins of the blind or their parents (John 9:2), we assign blame to injured parties themselves for the injuries that afflict them. Like Job's miserable counselors, we act and speak as if victims are their own perpetrators (Job 16:2). In the case of the poor, we might assume they are lazy, have a bad work ethic, or have made poor choices. Otherwise, why would they be poor? *I worked hard and applied myself to get where I am. Why won't they do the same?*

Not only is this way of thinking callous and cruel; it fails logic and defies experience. If we think this way about the poor, we are missing something fundamental to our calling as Christians. If this is how we think, we must repent of how selfish and dismissing and unloving we are being to our neighbors in need. For to condemn the poor is to condemn Jesus. Why?

Because Jesus was poor.

Moreover, when we condemn or disregard the poor for being

poor, we fail to recognize that there are whole systems that contribute to some people being born into a slum or gang-infested neighborhood or abusive home, even as others are born into a world of wealth and support and opportunity. Though the inequalities and injustices of the world's system undeniably privilege some and oppress others, we act as if the playing field is level for all people. We act as if each man, woman, and child—regardless of their situation—is fully responsible for their own destiny.

"If people work hard and apply themselves, things will turn out well for them," we may think to ourselves. Maybe so. And maybe not. Would we say such things to a boy whose mother is addicted to heroin? Or a single mother of six? Or a war-torn refugee living in the United States who knows no English and has no transferrable job skills?

To say such things would not inspire but rather defeat and trample on hearts. To say such things would be cruel.

Jesus tells us that more is expected of those who have been given much (Luke 12:48). So the proper question is, how much have we been given by God, and what does this mean with respect to our responsibility to our neighbors, especially those who are poor?

RECOGNIZING THE WORTH

There's still more to consider.

What if our lack of eagerness to "remember the poor" (Gal. 2:10) is because we don't see straight? What if, instead of being a burden, the poor are actually one of God's greatest gifts to us? What if the poor, like the couple who unknowingly gave more than anyone to a collection meant *for them*, are among our most competent teachers about what matters most in life, about how God's kingdom works, and about what we can carry with us when our present life comes to an end? What if the Macedonians have more to teach the Laodiceans than the Laodiceans have to teach the Macedonians? What if the widow's mite *is* indeed the greatest of all gifts that can be given? And what if all of these are indicative of the fact that we are all beggars, equally needy, equally impoverished, equally helpless? What if the greatest wealth is measured, not in terms of spreadsheets and bank accounts and properties and financial portfolios, but in terms of *feeling our scarcity* so deeply that we are led to find our true "net worth" not in what we've been able to accumulate for ourselves in this world, but in what God has given in an eternal inheritance that is "more precious than gold that perishes" and that is "imperishable, undefiled, and unfading, kept in heaven" for us (1 Peter 1:3–9)?

Once we begin to understand and experience "wealth" according to God's definition of the term—that *he himself* is our only true riches and that in comparison to him money is a small and insignificant thing—our perspective on the value of persons will be reoriented. Our hierarchies of who is important and who is expendable, of who is noteworthy and who is not-worthy, of who deserves our friendship and who does not, completely fade away. Because in God's economy, the poor in spirit—regardless of their so-called net worth—are the sole heirs of God's riches. "Blessed are the poor in spirit," Jesus said. Blessed are those who recognize that in having everything without Jesus, they have nothing, and in having Jesus and nothing else, they have everything. "For theirs is the kingdom of heaven" (Matt. 5:3).

Indeed, in the sight of God, a poor man is *worth* the same as a rich man. And so, in the name of Christ, our hierarchies must disappear. While this idea may be resisted by those who have much, it is irresistible to those who are accustomed to being overlooked and brushed aside.

These words from Bishop N. T. Wright can help us: "Don't let the world leave its dirty smudge on you. The world is always assessing people, sizing them up, putting them down, establishing a pecking order. And God, who sees and loves all alike, wants the church to reflect [his] generous, universal love in how it behaves."[7]

Similarly, Pope Francis is quoted as saying, "All life has inestimable value, even the weakest and most vulnerable, the sick, the old, the unborn, and the poor, are masterpieces of God's creation, made in his own image, destined to live forever, and deserving of the utmost respect and reverence."[8]

Every person is a masterpiece of God's creation. In truth, no person is a drain on the system or a burden to society. No people group can legitimately be dismissed or ignored or discarded or forgotten. All of us are *masterpieces*. All of us are crowns of God's creation, made just a little less than the angels and carriers of the divine imprint (Ps. 8:5–7).

Being poor is no more a sign of God's unhappiness than being rich is an indication of his favor. Material wealth is neither moral nor immoral—although the means of acquiring wealth is—and neither poverty nor riches is a sign of God's blessing nor a sign of God's curse.

So, could it be that in the same way that receiving *more* material wealth can bring relief to many who are poor, having *less* material wealth can bring relief to many who are rich? Maybe the blessing of doing justly and loving mercy goes two ways instead of just one. Maybe a true blessing is received by those who *lose* net worth through acts of generosity and care just as much as it is received by others in need who *gain*.

Austrian businessman Karl Rabeder, after giving away his entire $5.3 million fortune to charity, said the following in an interview:

For a long time, I believed that more wealth and luxury automatically meant more happiness. . . . But over time a conflicting feeling developed. More and more I heard the words, "Stop what you're doing now—all this luxury and consumerism—and start your real life." I had the feeling I was working as a slave for things that I did not wish for or need. . . . It was the biggest shock in my life when I realized how horrible, soulless and without feeling the five-star lifestyle is. . . . We spent all the money you could possibly spend. But in all that time we had the feeling we hadn't met a single real person—that we were all just actors. The staff played the role of being friendly and [we] played the role of being important, and nobody was real.

Since giving away his entire fortune to charity, Rabeder said he has felt "free, the opposite of heavy."[9] It turns out that some of the world's biggest burdens are carried by the rich as well as the poor.

"Blessed are you who are poor," Jesus said, "for yours is the kingdom of God" (Luke 6:20).

Karl Rabeder helps us see that material wealth is not our salvation or the answer to all of life's problems. And Jesus, who himself was poor, helps us see that the poor are not merely objects of condescending pity or solely recipients of charity. On the contrary, the poor have something unique to offer to the rest of the world. The poor show us how to live without the deadly illusion of self-sufficiency. And as Jesus, who became poor for our sake, reminds us, it is only from a place of need that we can discover a freedom that is easy and light: "Come to me, all who labor and are heavy laden, and I will give you rest. Take my yoke upon you, and learn from me, for I am gentle and lowly in heart, and you will find rest for your souls. For my yoke is easy, and my burden is light" (Matt. 11:28–30).

Becoming involved with our neighbors who are poor can teach us—*all* of us—to remember that the only true salvation is the kind that comes from outside ourselves, one that results in the humble admission that we are not as strong and self-sufficient as we think we are. Being among the poor can teach us that in God's kingdom the way up is down, and that spiritual wealth can only be acquired from a place of spiritual bankruptcy. In the faces and stories of the weak and dependent, Jesus invites all who are weary to come to him for rest.

"Come, everyone who thirsts," says the prophet, "come to the waters; and he who has no money, come, buy and eat! Come, buy wine and milk without money and without price. . . . Listen diligently to me, and eat what is good, and delight yourselves in rich food" (Isa. 55:1–2).

As we blindly live as if material wealth is the ultimate "blessing" and material scarcity is the ultimate "curse," Jesus urges us to open our eyes and truly see. He shows us, both with his life and with his words, how we can so easily see things upside down instead of right-side up. For it was more the crooks and prostitutes and lepers and homeless and materially poor, and less the proud, self-sufficient, prestigious scribes and Pharisees, who were made to feel at home in Christ's kingdom.

Indeed, it is more difficult for the rich to enter the kingdom of God—the realm of true blessedness—than it is for a camel to pass through the eye of a needle. And yet, what is impossible for man is possible with God, if our hearts can receive it (Matt. 19:24–26).

As the great old hymn reminds us, "All the fitness he requires is to feel your need of him."[10]

CHAPTER 8

EMBRACING WORK
AS MISSION

AS A PASTOR, I AM often surprised by the number of Christians who treat their "Monday" as if it has zero connection with their "Sunday." Many head into the world without a well-developed, biblically informed, game-changing outlook on the way life in Christ is meant to transform their vocational lives. This is not only a missed opportunity, but also a significant miscarriage of true Christian discipleship and mission.[1]

Christians operating with a sense of joy, purpose, and mission in their work are integral components of irresistible faith. When our own employees, colleagues, and bosses begin to see the impact of the gospel on the way we do our work, a new and needed dimension is added to our calling as "salt and light" in the world.

Of all people, Christians have a strong basis for this vision for work-as-mission: *Because Christ worked tirelessly and joyfully for our rescue, restoration, and renewal through his life, death, burial, and resurrection, we now have the greatest reason to work toward the rescuing, restoring, and renewing of God's world.* Ideally, this understanding of Christ's work on our behalf should compel us toward an exemplary work ethic, a zeal for producing a quality of work that will honor Christ, a life-giving posture toward all who are affected by our work, and a joyful drive to grow into our best creative and redemptive potential.

Such a vision for our work is compelling, yet there are factors that make its realization seem out of reach.

WHAT THE WHOLE WORLD WISHES FOR

If the whole world could wish for just one thing, what do you think it would be? Would it be peace and happiness? Financial security? A strong marriage? Well-adjusted children? Good health? What would *you* wish for?

A recent Gallup poll revealed the number-one thing that the world's five billion working-age people want. What the world wants even more than food, shelter, safety, and peace is a good, meaningful job. According to a related article:

> Gallup defines a good job as one with 30+ hours of work a week with a consistent paycheck from an employer. A *great* job is a job in which you believe your boss cares about your development, you can use your strengths every day at work, and you believe your work makes a contribution to something. So, your job matters and, subsequently, your *life* matters.[2]

Yet, despite this universal desire for a good job, work remains a conundrum to most of the world's population. In fact, there seems to be a global crisis related to work. According to another Gallup poll, most people in the world deeply dislike what they do for a living. A full 87 percent of those who *do* have work describe themselves as disengaged from and miserable in their jobs.[3]

In the film *Office Space*, the main character, Peter, enlists a hypnotherapist to help him with his lack of motivation and disdain toward his mundane, midlevel job. In a session with the therapist, he recounts a distressing realization:

> So, I was sitting in my cubicle today and I realized, ever since I started working, every single day of my life has been worse than the day before it. So that means that every single day that you see me, that's the worst day of my life.[4]

We might assume since Peter feels stuck in a midlevel job and is confined to a cubicle every day that his misery is a byproduct of his position on the org chart. But this kind of vocational dissatisfaction isn't just something that happens to those who aren't in charge. Many whom the world defines as "successful" and "at the top of their game" also experience deep disappointment in their work. This is true now and has been for millennia, as these words from a writer with great worldly success attest: "What has a man from all the toil and striving of heart with which he toils beneath the sun? For all his days are full of sorrow, and his work is a vexation. Even in the night his heart does not rest" (Eccl. 2:22–23).

Unlike Peter from *Office Space*, the ancient writer of Ecclesiastes had succeeded by virtually every earthly standard. He had created great works, built enormous houses, planted fruitful gardens, and provided lovely parks for his community (Eccl. 2:4–11). He was a picture of the self-made man, a paragon of prosperity, advancement, fame, fortune, and worldly greatness. And yet, even from this place, the self-made man of Ecclesiastes described his experience as one of "vexation." To be vexed is to be troubled, annoyed, irritated, peeved. Vexation is a deep distress or angst. This self-made man—rather than being deeply satisfied in the process and outcomes of his work—resented his toil, experienced despair, and spoke of his life as empty and vain, in many ways *because* of his work (Eccl. 2:17–26).

NAVIGATING VALLEYS
INSIDE THE VALLEY

In 2015, *Business Insider* magazine published an article about Markus Persson. Persson, the creator of the wildly successful video game *Minecraft*, sold his company for $2.5 billion—establishing him as one of the richest, most successful entrepreneurs in our time. Following the sale, he purchased a mansion for $70 million and spent his days living the dream with lavish parties, high-end vacations, world travel, and frequent hobnobbing with well-known celebrities.

At the peak of his success, when he seemed to be one of the world's happiest and most secure human beings, Persson shared the following Ecclesiastes-like reflections on his Twitter page: "The problem with getting everything is you run out of reasons to keep trying. Hanging out with a bunch of friends and partying with famous people, able to do whatever I want, and I have never felt more isolated."[5]

Not long ago, a friend sent me an essay about the work culture in Silicon Valley indicating that Markus Persson is by no means alone in his struggle. The writer, who had spent a good bit of time with successful start-up innovators and organization leaders in the tech industry, said that while Silicon Valley may be awash in material wealth, its workers are afflicted with a different kind of human poverty. This kind of poverty doesn't suffer materially as much as it suffers relationally, spiritually, and emotionally from the effects of personal ambition, ruthless competition, inhumane work hours, envy of those who are above them on the org chart, and a feeling of never having enough. These are, in the words of the writer, Silicon Valley's "working-class millionaires," who, in spite of having piles and piles of cash at their disposal, feel very insecure about their presumed *lack* of wealth.[6]

Similarly, reflecting on her newfound fame and fortune as a member of the pop music group Destiny's Child, Michelle Williams said, "I'm in one of the top-selling female groups of all time, suffering with depression. When I disclosed it to our manager at the time, bless his heart, he was like, 'You all just signed a multi-million-dollar deal. You're about to go on tour. What do you have to be depressed about?'"[7]

The point is this: Whether our work happens in a midlevel cubicle or in a corner office, whether it earns us zero dollars or billions of dollars, whether it plunges us into obscurity or puts us in front of adoring fans night after night, the *Office Space*, Ecclesiastes, Markus Persson, Michelle Williams, and Silicon Valley examples are going to hit close to home for many of us. And it gets tricky, because it is not merely our failures at work, but also our response to our successes that can lead to feelings of anticlimax, vexation, meaninglessness, and even despair.

Why on earth, especially when we experience success relative to the rest of the world, do we feel this way? Is it because our work itself isn't meaningful? Is it because we work too little or too much? Is it because we aren't living up to our true potential?

Or is it because our perspective about work lacks a redemptive and creative—or *biblically shaped*—imagination?

British writer Dorothy Sayers says it's the latter, and that the Church is largely at fault for this crisis. According to Sayers, rather than foster a robust vocational imagination in its people, the Church has allowed work and religion to become separate, and in many ways mutually exclusive, nonintersecting categories:

In nothing has the Church so lost Her hold on reality as Her failure to understand and respect the secular vocation. She has allowed work and religion to become separate departments, and is astonished to find that, as a result, the secular work of the world is turned to purely selfish and destructive ends, and that the greater part of the world's intelligent workers have become irreligious or at least uninterested in religion. . . . But is it astonishing? How can anyone remain interested in a religion that seems to have no concern with nine-tenths of his life?[8]

Based on Sayers's assessment, we must ask, "What does our work have to do with our faith, and what does our faith have to do with our work?" This question should be applied to *all* the work we do, whether volunteer or for hire, whether at home or in an office or out in the community or behind a lectern or on a stage or with our hands in the dirt.

A related question might be, "If good work is what the whole world wants most, if most of the world is deeply dissatisfied at work, and if Christians seem no different because they see such little connection between their faith and their work, then can we really expect the world to say of us, 'Their faith has an irresistible quality to it'?"

If the vast majority of people, including Christians, are unmotivated, disengaged, frustrated, and bored in their work, what is going on beneath the surface? Furthermore, can anything be done about it? Could there be a more fulfilling, life-giving, God-and-neighbor-loving way forward?

The first and most essential step is to recover a biblically informed imagination regarding work. But whether or not we have access to faith-work integration resources in our own local context, it is important for Christians especially to view work as central and not peripheral to our humanity, and especially to our life in Christ.

Think about it. If most of us spend forty or more waking hours each week—or eighty thousand hours in our lifetimes—devoted to work of some kind, how could we *not* consider how those hours are affected by our identity as followers of Christ and how our work impacts the world?

THE REASON FOR WORK

Scripture is clear on this. Human beings *need* to work because work is in our blood. As carriers of the divine imprint, as bearers of the image of God, we are, by nature and design, helplessly *vocational* beings.

Have you ever considered that the very first thing God—in whose image we are made—reveals about himself in the Bible is that he, God, is a worker? "In the beginning, God created . . ." That's right. God, the Maker of all things, launched the work-week by creating on day one water, soil, and sky, all designed as hospitable spaces for life. In subsequent days he made plants, land creatures, birds, fish, and then the crown of his creation—man and woman. Then, at the end of his work, God looked at everything he had made and called it very good (Gen. 1:31). You might say that God took great pride in his work.

But work did not stop with God. After creating everything, God put Adam and Eve in his garden and told them to work it and tend to it, to cultivate it . . . to become makers of culture— curators and caregivers for the advancement and flourishing of people, places, and things—as they exercised dominion on God's behalf over the world that God made and loves (Gen. 2:15). It is no small thing that when God identified work as essential to the human experience, he did so *before* the fall and the curse happened, not after. There was work in Paradise and it was good. And good it remains.

Work, all productive activity apart from rest and play, contributes to our fulfillment as God's image-bearers. It is one of the primary ways we have been invited by God to participate in his mission to redeem, restore, and develop the world.

Tim Keller, who has done a great deal to help the Christian imagination regarding faith and work, is fond of saying that history—*his*-story—began in a garden and ends in a city. In Eden, the garden of God's delight, there is an immense potential that is yet to be realized. So God tells the man and woman to take the raw material he has given and tend to it, develop it, and curate it: "Be fruitful and multiply and fill the earth and subdue it" (Gen. 1:28).

At the end of history, we are given a different picture, a more complete and developed one, in which everything has culminated in the new heaven and new earth, including the New Jerusalem—the Holy City of God (Rev. 21:1–2).

Why are these two bookends of God's history and ours—Eden and the New Jerusalem—so significant? Because this unfolding suggests that we live in a world that's under development, a world that's heading somewhere. Likewise, it suggests that all creative and restorative work that we do in that world—no matter how big or small—represents a purposeful contribution to the cosmic mission of God: "Therefore, my beloved brothers, be steadfast, immovable, always abounding in the work of the Lord, knowing that in the Lord your labor is not in vain" (1 Cor. 15:58).

I often remind our church family that their daily work is just as much God's work as is the work of missionaries and pastors. To repeat Dorothy Sayers's point, the sacred and secular must never be seen as separate from the vantage point of a Christian. Every bit of this *entire* world—church and missions, government, the social sector, family and home, business, healthcare, athletics, the arts and entertainment, and so on—is our Father's world. Every square inch of it! Therefore, every square inch of this world should benefit from the irresistible presence of Christ's followers, who endeavor to promote flourishing as Christ's aroma in every good industry and sector. As he did with Adam and Eve, God also has entrusted to us the responsibility of loving, serving, and blessing the world through our work.

In addition, because we bear God's image, work is necessary for our flourishing and also for the fulfillment of our calling as God's workers in God's world. The fall of Adam and Eve that ruined everything—relationships, nature, and work—had not happened yet. Work, in other words, is part of the ideal human existence, part of God's original (and eventual) *Paradise*. We cannot and will not fully flourish unless we are doing creative or restorative work that mirrors the work of God, the consummate Creator and Restorer. We cannot and will not fully flourish unless we become personally invested in the universal Christian job description—to use our time, energy, imagination, and resources to leave God's world better than we found it.

If you've ever wondered why children instinctively "get to work" each day with crayons and paper or with a pile of blocks or Legos, if you've ever wondered why retiring from a career rarely brings greater fulfillment to the retiree, this is the reason. We are wired to mirror God through creation and restoration, and in so doing to leave people, places, and things better than we found them.

THE GLORY AND DIGNITY OF ALL WORK

For those who question the value of their work, it is essential to see that every kind of work that creates something new or enhances something broken or lacking is glorious because of how it intersects with God's ongoing creative mission in the world. It is glorious because of how it further nudges God's Garden toward becoming the Holy City it's destined to be. But how do we determine whether our vocational endeavors are genuinely good endeavors?

The answer to this question is simple. Any kind of work that leaves people, places, or things in better shape than before—*any* kind of work that helps the city of man become more like the City of God where truth, beauty, goodness, order, and justice reign—is work that should be celebrated as good. This includes good work done by Christians. It also includes good work done by those who are not Christians.

Consider music. Creating music involves taking the raw material of sounds and words and fashioning them into a cohesive whole.[9] When carefully arranged, previously disconnected, random sounds and words have potential to add order to our lives, bring us more deeply in touch with reality, stir our souls, heal our wounds, and give us hope. Even Nietzsche, whose worldview was predominantly dark and cynical, said that in music "the passions enjoy themselves"[10] and "without music, human life would be a mistake."[11]

Consider the vocation of parenting. Fathers and mothers shape their children physically, emotionally, spiritually, cognitively, and in so many other ways. Sadly, our culture often diminishes this strong, sacrificial calling. Parenting, especially for a stay-at-home mom or dad, can often be an undervalued and overlooked vocation. However, such work without pay can be just as meaningful and valuable as the most economically profitable, high-profile occupation. Parenting is a good and beautiful and necessary work in its own right, and must be honored and esteemed along with all other vocational callings. Remember, God saw fit to include in his Ten Commandments the importance of giving due honor to mothers and fathers (Ex. 20:12). The American journalist and activist Dorothy Day recognized this in relation to her own calling as a mother. Reflecting on the birth of her daughter, she wrote, "If I had written the greatest book, composed the greatest symphony, painted the most beautiful painting or carved the most exquisite figure I could not have felt the more exalted creator than I did when they placed my child in my arms."[12]

Consider custodial work. Several years ago, I met a man named Joe. We asked each other several get-to-know-you questions, including, "So, what do you do?" Joe responded in a way I will never forget. He said, "I just push a broom."

What? *Just?* He just pushes a broom? Who in the world told him that he should ever say or think "just" with regard to his work?

What would the world be like without custodians, or for that matter caregivers, shelf-stockers, repairmen and women, mothers and fathers, seamstresses, busboys, police officers, data entry staff, construction workers, mechanics, and others who, though their jobs may be lower in profile and pay, make such an important, necessary impact that the world would not be able to function without them?

Jesus' chosen earthly vocation also illustrates the value and esteem due to those whose work may be, in relative terms, lower in prestige and pay. Many wanted to make Jesus into an earthly king, yet he chose instead to serve God and neighbor chiefly as a woodworker, a servant, a teacher, and a healer. That says something important about our absurd societal hierarchies that suggest some jobs are important and other jobs are not.

And what about the dignity of Joe and his work? Regarding Joe's work and all work, there are two statements (actual source unknown) that are deeply important:

The maid who sweeps her kitchen is doing the will of God just as much as the monk who prays—not because she may sing a Christian hymn as she sweeps but because God loves clean floors.

The Christian shoemaker does his Christian duty not by putting little crosses on the shoes, but by making good shoes, because God is interested in good craftsmanship.

Consider the story about President John F. Kennedy's visit to NASA Space Center in 1962. During his visit, he noticed a man who was carrying a broom. Pausing from his tour, the president approached the man and said, "Hi. I'm Jack Kennedy. What are you doing?"

"Well, Mr. President," the janitor said, "I'm helping put a man on the moon."

The NASA janitor understood the truth about all work, and especially his work. He wasn't just pushing a broom. He was making history.[13]

History began in a garden and will end in a city. Every vocation is a calling from God (the word itself comes from the Latin word *vocare*, which means "call") to nudge the Garden toward becoming an irresistible, life-giving City that we have been made to inhabit. And as we participate in this unfolding through our work, we don't do *just* anything. We make history.

RETHINKING THE MEANING OF MISSION

Writer and theologian Frederick Buechner said that our work is an essential part of our calling and that every good job exists on some level because the world needs for the work to be done. "The place God calls you to," Buechner wrote, "is the place where your deep gladness and the world's deep hunger meet."[14]

We participate in *God's* work through *our* work. And in this, we actively participate in executing God's creative and restorative work in the world. As the image of God, every time we participate in work that creates and restores, we also participate in God's work of leaving people, places, and things better.

How is this so? Mothers extend the nurture of God; artists and entrepreneurs, the creativity of God; government leaders and business executives, the rule of God; healthcare professionals and counselors, the healing hand of God; educators, the wisdom and knowledge of God; nonprofit workers, the mercy and compassion of God; fashion inventors and stylists, the beauty of God; attorneys and judges, the justice of God; marketers and advertisers, the evangelistic energy of God; authors and storytellers and filmmakers, the drama of God.

Our irresistible faith reflects the irresistibility of God himself, in all his facets, creativity, and passions, through the work that God has given us to do in the world.

Are we able to see that every good vocation is just as much a part of God's mission in the world as the vocations of pastor and missionary? What if we began to rethink "missions" altogether? In addition to commissioning pastors and missionaries for God's work, we can also commission artists, physicians, homemakers, educators, baristas, athletes, parents, intercessors, attorneys, landscapers, and salespeople.

Madeleine L'Engle said, "There is nothing so secular that it cannot be sacred, and that is one of the deepest messages of the Incarnation."[15]

Similarly, Nashville Institute for Faith and Work executive director Missy Wallace recently reminded me that Jesus spent more of his adult life working as a carpenter than he did in more formal public ministry. Furthermore, most of the thousands of people who listened to Jesus' teaching *stayed* in their existing vocations versus "going into the ministry."

So please, never say or think "just" about your or anyone else's work, as if it were somehow lesser in significance and value than other vocations. Perhaps this, too, is what makes Christianity irresistible in the eyes of those like the disciples, almost all of whom were without a formal higher education and whose jobs were less famous and lucrative. *In the gospel, just as every person is equal in significance to other people, so every vocation is equal in significance to other vocations.*

THE GROAN OF OUR WORK

We've already seen that God, after completing his work of creation, looked at what he had made and said it was very good. God looked at his work and celebrated. He was satisfied. And because God put his image in us, we, too, are wired to take pride in our work.

But something is also undeniably wrong. Unlike God in his work of creation, we fail our work and our work fails us. Due to lack of motivation and skill and capacity, we struggle to produce the kind of work that will truly satisfy us. Even with our best work, the enjoyment sours when someone or something comes along and spoils it. Cars break down, children choose foolishly, parishioners sin against God and each other, lawns grow weeds, roofs leak, food rots, investments flop, the best songs don't get cut or played, bodies age and get ill and/or injured.

There are theological reasons for this reality. Ever since Adam and Eve sought independence from God, work, just like every other good thing in God's creation, has been under a curse. God said to Adam, "Cursed is the ground because of you; in pain you shall eat of it . . . thorns and thistles it shall bring forth for you. . .

By the sweat of your face you shall eat bread, till you return to the ground" (Gen. 3:17–19).

Because of this cosmic curse, even people with wonderful jobs experience frustration and anticlimax in their work. Always seeming to envision more than we are able to accomplish, we become stuck . . . stuck between our innate, primal need to work and our inability to do it fully and to sustain it for the long haul. This explains the frustration of the writer of Ecclesiastes, the boredom and malaise of Peter in *Office Space*, the depression and loneliness of Markus Persson, and the dissatisfaction of Silicon Valley millionaires mentioned earlier in this chapter.

In a sense, we are all like Sisyphus, the mythological Greek character whose story doesn't seem like a myth at all. Because of selfish ambition and deceitfulness, Sisyphus was condemned to eternal punishment. His sentence consisted of rolling a large, heavy rock to the top of a hill. Whenever he got close to the top, the rock would roll back down the hill. For the rest of eternity, he was doomed to repeat this frustrating task.

Do you ever identify with Sisyphus at your work? Stuck in frustration and anticlimax, caught in the curse pronounced on work after Adam's fall (Gen. 3:17–19), do you ever feel that you've been doomed like Sisyphus? Perhaps it's true. Perhaps we've all lost our irresistible vocational vigor because we've been condemned to a lifetime of hard work that will be met, at the end of each futile effort, with a rock rolled back down to the bottom of a hill.

Or perhaps a bigger, brighter, more hopeful story is being told behind the scenes in relation to our work—a story that can provide hope and even the flourishing of irresistible faith brought to bear on work that may appear mundane, fruitless, and pointless. Could this even be possible?

THE FRUSTRATED WORK OF JESUS

The Bible gives us a clear example of someone whose life's work seemed to result in nothing but failure:

Jesus.

Jesus was a unique leader to be sure—the *flawless* leader who never erred in his motives or mission. He poured all that he had into his twelve disciples over a period of three solid years. But at the end of those three years, Judas sold him out for a small bag of coins, Peter renounced him three times publicly, and every single one of those disciples abandoned him in his darkest hour. How must Jesus, as the architect and perfecter of faith, have felt each time he used the term "you of little faith" in reference to the disciples into whom he had poured so much of his life and energy? And how must he have felt about having only 120 followers *after* he rose from the dead and appeared to over 500 people (Acts 1:15; 1 Cor. 15:6)?

It turns out that even Jesus, the one with enough power to speak the galaxies into existence, had to endure the Sisyphus experience in *his* work of saving souls and loving people, places, and things to life. As irresistible as he is, the world still resisted him, quite literally, to the death. Shouldn't we, who are far less strong and far less perfect than he, expect similar frustration ourselves? If Jesus, who will one day resolve every groan in his good creation, was subject to the groan, shouldn't we expect to be also?

And yet, if the story of Scripture also represents the unfolding story of God and his universe, we can take comfort in knowing that the Story's final chapter has not yet begun for us. In fact, we currently live inside what amounts to a single sentence in a single paragraph in a single chapter of God's Book—a sentence that, in many aspects of our work, represents the groan more than it represents flourishing, life, and peace. However, the best is yet to come.

GOD'S FUTURE AND THE HEALING
OF CREATION'S GROAN

One time, J. R. R. Tolkien wrote a short story to help him process his own frustration with work. The story, "Leaf by Niggle," was about an artist who had been commissioned to paint a mural on the side of city hall. Niggle spent the rest of his career attempting to complete that mural, a large and colorful tree that would inspire for years to come. But in the end, the artist was only able to paint one single leaf. And then he died. On the train to heaven, Niggle saw a vague but familiar image in the distance. He asked the conductor to stop the train immediately. When Niggle got off, he approached the object and discovered that it was a tree—his tree—complete and lovelier than he had ever imagined. And there, in the middle of the tree, was his contribution—Niggle's leaf for the whole world to see. In the end, Niggle discovered that all of it, the tree and even his single leaf, was a glorious, completed gift.

Tolkien wrote "Leaf by Niggle" as a way to process his frustration with another work of his, one that he had spent years creating but despaired would never be completed or appreciated by anyone. This was his creation of Middle-earth, which the world came to know through *The Lord of the Rings*.

If only Tolkien had known then what we know now about his "unsuccessful" work. And if only we knew now what we will one day know about our own work and how it fits into God's overall plan to save and heal the world. Perhaps then we would begin feeling an irresistible draw *toward* the work God has given us to accomplish in his world versus being drawn away from it into frustration, boredom, or even despair.

In those moments when you are tempted to stop pressing on and to give up, in those moments when you might be tempted to use the word *just* about your work, I encourage you to visit, and then revisit, the story of "Leaf by Niggle." I encourage you to consider not only the past but also the future, where the significance of *your* life's work, which may seem like only a leaf or two, will be revealed as an essential part of the tree that God will place right in the middle of *his* City—the great Tree of Life, which will be for the healing of the nations (Rev. 22:2).

Although it is sometimes hard to believe that your work, done for God's glory, has enduring significance, it absolutely does. In their book *Every Good Endeavor*, Tim Keller and Katherine Alsdorf do a tremendous job of explaining the significance of Niggle's leaf and how it relates to our present stories:

> There really is a tree. Whatever you are seeking in your work—the city of justice and peace, the world of brilliance and beauty, the story, the order, the healing, it is there. There is a God, there is a future healed world that He will bring about and your work is showing it (in part) to others. Your work will only be partially successful on your best days, in bringing that world about. But inevitably, that whole tree that you see—the beauty, the harmony, justice, comfort, joy and community—will come to fruition. If you know all this, you will not be despondent that you can only get a leaf or two out of this life. You will work with satisfaction and joy.[16]

These comments from Tim and Katherine help me see that my work, whether I or anyone else recognizes it or not, fits in as an essential, glorious "leaf" on *God's* glorious tree.

Scripture promises, "No eye has seen, nor ear heard, nor the heart of man imagined, what God has prepared for those who love him" (1 Cor. 2:9). It also promises that the good work he has begun in us, every good work—whether it be the work of becoming more like Jesus in our character, or the work of painting just a leaf when we dream of a tree—will be completed. The God who is creator and restorer and architect and builder of his great city will be faithful to complete that work (Phil. 1:6). And as he completes that work, he will also look toward us through the finished work of Jesus and say, "Well done, good and faithful servant" (Matt. 25:23).

Child of God, the good work that you do now will go on into eternity. It's a leaf on the Creator's tree that contains a beauty and uniqueness that will, in its finished form, become an irresistible addition to the True Artist's everlasting tree.

Don't ever forget that in every good work you do, you are putting a man on the moon and you are making history.

And as you take heart in these things, pray earnestly and often that God will use your contributions in such a way that a watching world will see your good works and glorify your Father in heaven (Matt. 5:15–16).

CHAPTER 9

LEAVING IT BETTER

AS WE HAVE SEEN IN previous chapters, irresistible faith must be undergirded by a shared commitment among Christians to join a movement—specifically, *God's* movement in Christ—of loving people, places, and things to life.

Any movement that leads to irresistible faith—any movement that has promise for turning us into the kind of Christians the world can't resist—must begin with a transformation in our own hearts and lives. This "new creation" movement happens as the Holy Spirit takes up residence in us, reminding us daily through his Word how loved and kept we are in Christ and forming us into more life-giving people. As this personal transformation occurs, we are likewise drawn into community with others who share this vision for irresistible faith. And then, together, we turn our faces outward to the world that God so loves, accepting his generous invitation to include us in his good work.

My hope is that the preceding pages have sparked something in you that makes you want to be part of this kind of movement. In these last pages, I would first like to demonstrate how any movement that attempts to leave the world better *without the undergirding of Jesus and his gospel of grace* will instead actually leave the world worse. For what Jesus said to his followers over two thousand years ago, he also says to us today: "Apart from me you can do nothing" (John 15:5).

And yet, it is not uncommon that we humans—believing so deeply in our own intelligence, skillfulness, ingenuity, and savvy—fail to embrace this truth from Jesus as being self-evident.

TOO SOPHISTICATED FOR OUR OWN GOOD?

Have you ever felt wildly optimistic about an idea or a movement with so much promise and momentum that failure seemed impossible . . . and then failure happened?

The twentieth-century British writer and social commentator H. G. Wells experienced such a failure with the secular humanist worldview he had once championed. Early in his career, rooted in a post-Enlightenment perspective on the promise of social engineering, Wells wrote in 1937 that it was only a matter of time before the human race achieved the utopian world that past generations had only dreamed about:

> Can we doubt that presently our race will more than realize our boldest imaginations, that it will achieve unity and peace, and that our children will live in a world made more splendid and lovely than any palace or garden than we know, going on from strength to strength in an ever-widening circle of achievement?[1]

As H. G. Wells wrote these hopeful words about human goodness and progress, Adolf Hitler was rising to power in Germany and his murderous agenda was gaining disturbing momentum. Stalin was on a similar course, and Japan and China were at war with each other. After World War II, Wells was confronted by a world that was deeply broken and a humanity that showed few signs of moral improvement. Wells underwent a radical shift from optimism and hope to pessimism and despair. Reflecting on the cruel atrocities he had witnessed, he observed that events had "come near to breaking [his] spirit altogether."[2]

Aldous Huxley, the British social critic and Wells's contemporary whose 1931 dystopian novel *Brave New World* both popularized and satirized the secular humanist utopian vision, would descend to an even more cynical posture in his final years. "Maybe," Huxley is quoted as saying, "this planet is another planet's hell."[3] On his deathbed in 1963, afflicted with cancer and too weak to utter words or sentences, Huxley handed a written note to his wife that read, "LSD, 100 mg."[4]

Considering how two intellectuals like Wells and Huxley could begin with such great optimism only to plummet into an abyss of cynicism and despair about people and the world and the future, one wonders how their initial optimism could later be so easily resurrected by some of the top academics of the late twentieth century.

In 1973, at the dawn of the technological boom, secular thinkers were once again enthusiastic about what human beings seemed poised to accomplish and become. From this collective spirit, the second *Humanist Manifesto* (the first had been released during the era of Wells and Huxley in 1933) was written. Signed by approximately 150 of the world's top secular academics—many of whom were disciples of Wells and Huxley—the second *Manifesto* presented a similar vision for human progress that included the following words:

> The next century *can be* and *should be* the humanistic century.
> Dramatic scientific, technological, and ever-accelerating social

and political changes crowd our awareness. We have virtually conquered the planet, explored the moon, overcome the natural limits of travel and communication; we stand at the dawn of a new age, ready to move farther into space and perhaps inhabit other planets. Using technology wisely, *we can* control our environment, conquer poverty, markedly reduce disease, extend our life-span, significantly modify our behavior, alter the course of human evolution and cultural development, unlock vast new powers, and provide humankind with unparalleled opportunity for achieving an abundant and meaningful life.[5]

Now, just a few decades later, it is an understatement to say that both the first and second *Manifestos* of secular humanism failed significantly to reach their goals. In spite of humanity's best and brightest efforts, the world is still plagued by violence, poverty, racism, economic inequality, greed, child neglect, loveless marriages, sex addiction, human trafficking, global hunger, political divisiveness, and ideological outrage. The current political climate has us jaded about public leadership of any kind. Technologies designed to build greater connectivity have left us, according to *Psychology Today*, lonelier and more depressed and with lower self-esteem.[6] Anxiety and depression are pervasive. So are online mob culture and shaming, teen bullying and suicide, pornography, prostitution, child abuse, fatherlessness, genocide, persecution, and terrorism.

It seems that the humanist project has left the world worse, not better.

Sensitive souls are left to wonder if there is any answer to the troubles that plague us. After all the advances in technology and research, what are we to make of a world that *still* seems more tired than energized, more hurting than whole, more sick than healthy, more life-sucking than life-giving, more divided than united, and more bent toward decline than toward progress? Furthermore, what, if anything, can be done about it? If the world's top thinkers and leaders can't succeed in moving the world in a more life-giving direction, who can?

JESUS' ANSWER TO THE WORLD'S WOES

According to Jesus, there is and always has been a group of ambassadors endowed with the resources to nudge the world toward peace, healing, wholeness, and flourishing. These ambassadors are unique. They are equipped to be less dependent on the strength of the human spirit, the intelligence of the human mind, and the moxie of the human will. They are called to lean instead on the strength of the Holy Spirit, the wisdom of God, and the determination of God's vision to bring about peace, health, wholeness, and flourishing.

Included among Jesus' ambassadors are academics and scientists and celebrities and politicians and movers and shakers and such, to be sure.

But in addition to these, Jesus also includes those *like himself* who aren't part of the world's elite clubs, VIP lists, and manifestos. These are people like Amos and Bathsheba and Peter and Mary the mother of Jesus, easily dismissed as "weak" and "common" and "foolish" and "low" and "despised," but who, time and time again, find themselves right in the center of God's strategy to bless and heal the world:

> For consider your calling, brothers: not many of you were wise
> according to worldly standards, not many were powerful, not
> many were of noble birth. But God chose what is foolish in the
> world to shame the wise; God chose what is weak in the world

to shame the strong; God chose what is low and despised in the world, even things that are not, to bring to nothing things that are, so that no human being might boast. . . Because of him you are in Christ Jesus, who became to us wisdom from God, righteousness and sanctification and redemption. (1 Cor. 1:26–30)

According to the One who created and sustains and intends to renew the world, the answer to the world's woes includes *ordinary* men, women, and children who have been awakened to their place in the Story of an extraordinary God.

Central to his plan to mend the world's woes, Jesus says, are *Christians of every kind.* To a mostly overlooked, uneducated, and noncredentialed—yet also redeemed, restored, forgiven, and Spirit-filled—band of fishermen, tax collectors, addicts, widows, children, and former prostitutes, Jesus spoke these words: "*You* are the salt of the earth. . . . *You* are the light of the world. A city set on a hill cannot be hidden. . . . Let your light shine before others, so that they may see your good works and give glory to your Father who is in heaven" (Matt. 5:13–14, 16, emphasis added). These three metaphors of salt, light, and city stir our imaginations about *our* role in God's mission to rescue and restore and enrich his world. But what did he mean by them?

THE UNIVERSAL JOB DESCRIPTION

Whatever one's place in life, whatever age or influence, all Christians are filled with the Holy Spirit's power, endowed with the Father's wisdom through Scripture, and energized by the love of Jesus. As such, all Christians are called as Christ's ambassadors into the places where they live, work, play, and worship, with the glorious purpose of *leaving people, places, and things better than they found them*. This is the universal Christian job description.

As a father of two daughters, I am often proud of them for their various ideas and endeavors. One such endeavor for our oldest daughter was to build a thriving babysitting business in her mid-teen years.

To give herself a competitive edge, our daughter decided that she would commit herself to two practices that, in her opinion, would make her services irresistible to the parents and children she served. First, she would resist the urge to be on her phone and social media and would instead actively engage and play with the kids until their bedtime. Second, after putting the kids to bed, she would tidy the house or apartment—especially the main living space, sink, and kitchen—so that when the parents arrived home, the house would be in better shape at the *end* of the evening than it was at the beginning.

Faithfully, our daughter committed herself to these two practices. Before long, she was getting so many babysitting opportunities that she had to start referring some parents to her friends. These two simple actions of playing with the kids and cleaning the home made her the favorite babysitter to the kids *and* the parents of virtually every family she served. Even now, when a break from college is on the horizon, parents will line up to "preorder" her babysitting services for the weeks she will be at home. You might say that she has positioned herself—from a consistent commitment to be fully present with *people* and to diligently care for *places* and *things*—to "enjoy the favor of all the parents."

In this seemingly small thing, our daughter provided an example for us of how irresistible faith can play out in the ordinary stuff of life. Christians both young and old are called to serve the world as engaged servants, fully present and always looking for opportunities to leave people, places, and things better than they found them. These endeavors don't have to take place on a grand stage. In fact, for most of us, opportunities exist in the daily, ordinary stuff of life. And yet, as Christians everywhere look for small ways to "leave it better," the collective impact can have potentially staggering effects. The environmentalist phrase "Think globally, act locally" applies marvelously to life in Christ. As each of us does our part and as a critical mass of irresistible faith forms in all the places where we live, work, and play, the potential for a better world and for God's kingdom to come on earth as it is in heaven—*through us*—becomes real.

Our daughter's intentionality about "leaving it better" and becoming an irresistible presence in every home she served as a babysitter was also the pervasive attitude among first-century Christians. These believers did not feel a need to become a powerful "moral majority" in order to impact the world around them, for they realized, as Jesus had clearly told them, that his kingdom is *not* of this world (John 18:36). Rather than controlling the world through coercive and politically partisan force, Jesus' method was to win the world through the persuasive power of kindness and neighbor-love.

Indeed, Jesus and his tribe of followers gained favor and influence by living among their neighbors and colleagues—including those who were poor, marginalized, and forgotten—as an intentional, creative, love-driven, and life-giving minority. As they freely gave to their neighbors the gift of love, service, and presence, they seized every opportunity to leave places and things better than they found them. It would be fair to say that if these Christians were taken out of the world, their neighbors would have sorely missed them.

A MISSED OPPORTUNITY
FOR CHRISTIANS?

Many of us in twenty-first-century America have let slip away this universal job description for living as a love-driven, life-giving minority. Rather than denying ourselves, taking up our crosses, and following Jesus, we instead deny our neighbors and take up our comforts, all in an attempt to protect our own interests and follow our personal dreams.

This tendency is especially apparent in light of Christ's call to generosity. In fact, many who identify as followers of Christ are functional atheists when it comes to money. Rather than "having money," for many people it's their money that has them . . . around the neck. This is a major inhibitor of the advancement of irresistible faith. Rather than spending ourselves for the world, many of us seem more bent on spending whatever we have been given on ourselves.

In his book *The Total Money Makeover,* my friend and Christian financial expert Dave Ramsey puts it this way: "We buy things we don't need with money we don't have to impress people we don't like."

Although Scripture establishes the tithe—10 percent of one's income—as the minimum amount believers are supposed to be giving to the ministry of their local churches,[7] according to theologian and social activist Ron Sider, the national average for *all* Christian charitable giving is a paltry 2.4 percent.[8] Brian Kluth, author and founder of a group called Maximum Generosity, theorizes about the reason for this reality:

> While some evangelicals are very generous, many are not. The concept that giving to God's work (local church, ministries/

missions, the needy) should be a person's highest financial priority is embraced by very few Christians in today's materialistic, consumer-driven, and debt-ridden society, even though Scripture is clear on this teaching. I feel that part of the problem is many churches have made their teaching focus on generosity being the "budget" instead of the Bible. . . . Budgets should be the spending plan, not the giving goal.[9]

What does this have to do with the cultivation of irresistible faith? It's simple. Wherever we are spending our money is usually where we are spending our lives. As Jesus said, "Where your treasure is, there your heart will be also" (Matt. 6:21). As Tim Keller notes in his book *Generous Justice,* "Christ literally walked in our shoes and entered into our affliction. Those who will not help others until [those others] are destitute reveal that Christ's love has not yet turned them into the sympathetic [or generous] persons the gospel should make them."[10]

Perhaps challenges like this from Keller can function as a clarion call to Christians to return to our roots and once again live as Jesus' ambassadors, aroma, and "sent ones" for the healing, restoration, and rejuvenation of our tired, sin-sick world. Now is the time to repent of the ways we have contributed *to* the world's sorrow and brokenness—whether by doing active harm or by passively doing nothing—versus seeking to be healing agents *of* the world's sorrow and brokenness.

BUT WHAT IF . . . ?

What if Christians everywhere were willing to consider a reworking of Dave Ramsey's statement above—not merely in written form, but also through our lives—so that a new narrative could be written? In other words, what if Christians, rather than buying things we don't need with money we don't have to impress people we don't like, instead began to deploy money (and time, energy, and mindshare) that we *do* have on things God has determined the world *does* need in order to love people whom *God* loves—to the end that God receives glory through our obedient, irresistible faith, and that in this, we receive our greatest joy?

What if . . . ?

What if, in the spirit of Jesus providing wine at a wedding feast (John 2:1–11) and of the audacious, forgiving father throwing a grand feast for the entire community (Luke 15:11–32), Christians became known for hosting hospitable, inclusive, and life-giving parties for friends, neighbors, colleagues, strangers, and strugglers (Matt. 22:1–14)?

What if, in the spirit of Paul intelligently and winsomely engaging Greek academics with the truth of the gospel, Christians became known for engaging in thoughtful, enriching, challenging, and honoring discourse about God, humanity, and life (Acts 17:22–34; Col. 4:6; 1 Peter 3:15)?

What if, in the spirit of the early church's care and provision for vulnerable children *and* women, women experiencing the trauma and fear of an unplanned pregnancy began to think first of local churches, not local clinics, as comprehensively life-giving places of comfort, counsel, and care (James 1:27)?

What if, in the spirit of Scripture's vision for marriage and sexuality, instead of condemning the world for its broken sexuality, Christians exemplified the beauty of biblical marriage by *having* biblical marriages—the countercultural kind in which mutual love, respect, and submission are tenderly shared between husbands and wives (Eph. 5:22–33)?

What if, as an answer to the loneliness felt by uncoupled men and women both inside and outside the church, Christians became known for nurturing communities in which every person, regardless of sexual orientation or marital status, is given the full experience of family (Matt. 12:49–50; Rom. 8:15)?

What if the local church became the world's answer to loneliness and isolation, thereby becoming the life-giving alternative to social media–induced isolation and depression, soul-stealing pornography habits, body-exploiting hookups, noncommittal cohabitations, and lonesome barstools (Ps. 68:6; 1 Cor. 7:7–8; Eph. 5:22–33)?

What if, in the spirit of Scripture's vision for the integration of faith and work, Christians became known as the bosses everyone wants to work for, the colleagues everyone wants to work alongside, and the employees everyone wants to hire (Eph. 6:5–9)?

What if, in the spirit of Scripture's vision for doing justly and loving mercy, Christians became widely known as the world's *first* and *most thorough* responders whenever a friend, neighbor, colleague, or stranger experiences tragedy, such as divorce, unemployment, a crippling diagnosis, a loved one's death, or a rebellious child (Micah 6:8)?

What if, in the spirit of the good Samaritan, Christians became widely known as those who rescue from danger, bandage wounds, and provide care and shelter to those who have been beaten, abandoned, and left for dead by the cruelty of human selfishness and greed (Luke 10:25–37)?

What if, in the spirit of Jesus' life and teaching, Christians became widely known not only as the best kind of friends, but as the best kind of enemies—responding to persecution with prayer, to scorn with kindness, to selfishness with generosity, to offense with forgiveness, and to hatefulness with grace and love (Matt. 5:1–12)?

What if, in the spirit of Jesus, Christians once again became known as those who welcome sinners and eat with them—such that sinners begin to say of Christians, "I like them, and I want to be like them" (Luke 15:1–2, 11–32)?

What if, in the spirit of the early church, Christians once again began to enjoy the favor of *all* the people—not because of how *like* the world they have become through assimilation and accommodation, but because of how *unlike* the world they have become through their lives of love and good deeds? What if Christians once again, collectively and comprehensively and universally, lived such compelling lives that the Lord added daily to their number those who were being saved (Acts 2:42–47)?

And what if—and this is ever so important in consideration of these other what-ifs—we realized that the pressure to make such things happen is completely *off* our shoulders because the ultimate responsibility and power for change has been placed squarely on *Jesus'* shoulders? Jesus, and only Jesus, holds the keys for unlocking the flourishing of the people, places, and things that he not only created but sustains and restores and will ultimately perfect in glory. "He comes to make *his* blessings flow, far as the curse is found."[11] And "of the increase of *his* government and of peace there will be no end" (Isa. 9:7, emphasis added).

Indeed, *we* are the salt of the earth, the city on a hill, and the light of the world—but the light we shine is *his* light and not our own—just as the moon, having no light of its own, nonetheless was created to reflect the light of the sun in such a way that it illuminates the darkness of night. His light is available to us every single day. All we have to do is walk outside, bask in it, and receive it.

While many what-ifs are indeed happening in communities and cities all over the world, there is still much progress to be made. There is still a need for the people of Jesus to place ourselves in the path of God's light so his light will reflect off us as it did from the face of Moses as he came down from the mountain (Ex. 34:29–35).

Said another way, as the secular humanist utopian vision and technological advances and partisan politics continue to *not* deliver on their promises, now is the time for Christians to reengage the promises of old, promises that envision a world fueled by trust, not in the human machine, but in the power that resides in the One who created the galaxies by breathing, the One who made a blind man see, and the One who brings dead people, dead places, and dead things back to life.

As Jesus promised to his disciples after commanding them to go out into all the world, preaching the gospel to all peoples, baptizing them in the name of the Father, Son, and Holy Spirit, and teaching them to obey all of Jesus' commands, "And behold, I am with you always, to the end of the age" (Matt. 28:16–20), and "I will never leave you nor forsake you" (Heb. 13:5).

As Saint Augustine once prayed, "Lord, command what you will and grant what you command!"[12] And this our Savior will surely do for us.

OF THOSE WHO HAVE BEEN GIVEN MUCH, MUCH IS EXPECTED

Throughout history many men and women of faith from positions of fame and power and influence, have left the world better on a national and global scale. These faithful, high-profile servants are much like the high-profile servants in Scripture—those with exceptional access to power and/or positions of power, such as Abraham, Joseph, Moses, Deborah, Ruth, David, Solomon, Nehemiah, Esther, Job, Daniel, Matthew, Nicodemus, Zacchaeus, and Paul. All stewarded their lives and influence in ways that honored Jesus' teaching, "Everyone to whom much was given, of him much will be required, and from him to whom they entrusted much, they will demand the more" (Luke 12:48).

Similarly, Jesus told a parable about the way he intends for us to invest our lives:

> "For [the kingdom of God] will be like a man going on a journey, who called his servants and entrusted to them his property. To one he gave five talents, to another two, to another one, to each according to his ability. Then he went away. He who had received the five talents went at once and traded with them, and he made five talents more. So also he who had the two talents made two talents more. . . . His master said to him, 'Well done, good and faithful servant. You have been faithful over a little; I will set you over much. Enter into the joy of your master.'" (Matt. 25:14–17, 21)

In his thought-provoking book *To Change the World*, University of Virginia sociologist James Davison Hunter says similar things. Hunter argues that those he calls "cultural elites"—those with access to and control of disproportionate amounts of money, power, networks, and influence—are in a unique position to be able to move the needle toward a better, truer, more just, and more beautiful world. Such men and women have a unique opportunity and responsibility to use what has been entrusted to them for good versus ill.[13]

Power, money, influence, and platform are not meant to be hoarded, nor are they meant to be used for selfish purposes. Rather, such "talents" are meant to be invested for King Jesus and his purposes toward a "return" that looks and feels more like the kingdom of God and less like the kingdom of self. Educators, broadcasters, journalists, politicians, authors, athletes, artists, entertainers, executives, and pastors alike should consider carefully Hunter's words:

> The deepest and most enduring forms of cultural change nearly always occur from the "top down." In other words, the work of

world-making and world-changing are, by and large, the work of elites: gatekeepers who provide creative direction and management within spheres of social life. Even where the impetus for change draws from popular agitation, it does not gain traction until it is embraced and propagated by elites.[14]

WHAT ABOUT US "REGULAR" FOLK?

Hunter's words raise a very important question: *What about those who have comparatively fewer "talents" to work with?* Jesus spoke not only to highly educated influencers like Paul, accomplished physicians like Luke, and wealthy government leaders like Matthew, but also to the lepers and recovering junkies, to the weak and wounded, to the outcasts, and to those struggling to make ends meet. He also spoke to "average" and less-public people, to blue-collar workers with calluses on their hands and feet, to those who caught fish for a living, to middle managers, and to regular moms and dads. In fact, in his sermons and parables, Jesus spoke more to regular folk than he did to those in the halls of power.

Although God's beloved family—as well as God's plan for leaving the world better—includes those with access to power and influence and celebrity, there are no special or "elite" classes of people in Christ's mission of loving people, places, and things to life.

His mission to love, serve, and renew the world is an all-inclusive proposition.

And? We *all* get to be part of it.

So, where shall we begin?

A PRAYER FOR
IRRESISTIBLE FAITH

TO BETTER KNOW YOUR GRACE, to better walk in community, and to better participate in *your* mission of loving people, places, and things to life, we pray for a faith that will cause the world to find in you an irresistible Lord and Savior.

Lord, hear our prayer.

We ask that you would shape us, your people, into a family united in Christ that aspires in all things to be led by Scripture. We ask that together, in our local contexts as well as from opposite sides of the globe, we, your people, would look to the Father's perfect Word as given in the Old and New Testaments to form our spiritual life. Help us look to Jesus, the Son of God and Savior of sinners, to forgive our sins, refresh our spirits, ignite our worship, and transform our characters. Ignite our hearts through the power of the Holy Spirit who indwells us, and whose power raised Jesus from the dead. Help us to live resurrected lives, loving you with our whole selves and our neighbor as ourselves.

Lord, hear our prayer.

We ask that because you have called and gathered Christ's

Church to be a family, you would lead us to share life with one another and not succumb to the temptation to go it alone. In our beliefs and teaching, help us unite around Scripture's essential truths, while promoting liberty around things about which Scripture is flexible or silent. In our worship, help us to honor you, to gather often around the Lord's Table, and to create belonging for one another and all whom you bring through our doors. In our life together, help us to honor one another above ourselves as we implement *your* vision for community—welcoming, listening to, loving, confessing to, forgiving, serving, comforting, sharing burdens with, caring and praying for, remaining loyal to, and spurring on the best in one another.

Lord, hear our prayer.

We ask that you would help us celebrate and increase our diversity—opening our lives and hearts and homes to sinners and saints, doubters and believers, seekers and skeptics, prodigals and Pharisees, young and old, married and unmarried, leaders and followers, famous and infamous, our own races and other races, happy and depressed, helpers and those who need help, creative and corporate, conservative and liberal, domestic and international, affluent and bankrupt, public and private and home schooled— and all others we may encounter. Help us to expand our "us"[1] by carefully listening to, learning from, and being shaped by one another's unique experiences and perspectives.

Lord, hear our prayer.

As a church rooted in Jesus Christ—who taught that it is more blessed to give than it is to receive and that greatness is found through serving—please help us to give ourselves away with an irresistible generosity. Help us to see that our "conservative" belief that every word of Scripture is right and good and true will compel us toward "liberal" lives of generosity and love. Help us daily to live not only for ourselves but as partakers in a movement of your self-donating kingdom. Because you love us, you include us—along with all your children everywhere—in your mission of loving people, places, and things to life. Because we are your beloved ambassadors, you send us out to "so love the world" with the goal of leaving the world better than we found it. Please include us in your good work, helping us to add such irresistible value to our cities and towns and neighborhoods that if Christians disappeared, our cities and towns and neighborhoods would weep.

Lord, hear our prayer.

Because you have called us to let our light shine before men that they may see our good deeds and glorify our Father in heaven, help our faith to be a public faith with an irresistible quality to it. Help us love and serve all our neighbors in the places where we live, work, and play. Lead us into all sorts of civil conversations that unite believers, seekers, and nonbelievers around shared interests, in hopes that your truth, beauty, love, and justice will be brought to bear on the most central and pressing issues of our time. Like the longing father in Luke 15, give us a vision for hosting life-giving, grace-drenched parties—not only for ourselves but also for all our neighbors. Let us become a sign of your kingdom and of how heaven rejoices when prodigals come home and when cynics lay down their defenses and join the celebration.

Lord, hear our prayer.

We ask that you would help us to befriend those who do not believe as we do. Show us what it means to welcome all people into our worship services, parties, conversations, homes, and lives, including those who have misgivings or doubts about the beliefs, ethics, generosity, self-denial, and countercultural nature of historic Christianity.

Lord, hear our prayer.

As Christ's ambassadors to our neighbors in need, please help us live irresistible lives of mercy and justice. Shape us into the kinds of people who, because you came to us in *our* dire need and rescued us, give special attention to, and generously channel our resources toward, improving conditions and systems—whether spiritual, social, economic, or vocational—for the poor, immigrants and refugees, ethnic and other minorities, and others who lack resources, opportunity, or privilege. Help us embrace the idea that as conditions improve for those who have power, conditions must also improve for those who lack power, and never at their expense. For wealth, privilege, and power are given to be stewarded and shared for the benefit of all, not protected and kept merely for the benefit of some.

Lord, hear our prayer.

As those who have been called into the world by you to serve you in our work, please help us eliminate the false dichotomy of sacred versus secular. Help us live in such a way that affirms that every good work—whether creative or restorative—is no less *your* work than the work of pastors and missionaries. Grant us the ability and resources to be able to train and equip Christians to integrate their faith and their work. Help Christians to become irresistible leaders, not only in church, but also in business, education, the social sector, the arts and entertainment, government, media, and other channels of influence. Help us to approach our work with tenacity, purpose, and confidence that our work contributes meaningfully to your mission to heal, restore, and develop the world.

Lord, hear our prayer.

Finally, because your kingdom is much greater than a single church or community or municipality, we will pray and work for the flourishing of all people and not just our people; of all churches and not just our church; of all cities and not just our city; and of all nations and not just our nation. Help us to see and embrace opportunities to share our resources and capital—whether spoken, written, creative, financial, relational, professional, or otherwise—toward your vision to bless and heal the world. As you help us do this, help us also to celebrate wherever, whenever, and through whomever you choose to build your kingdom. Please grant us humility and gratitude, that we might not concern ourselves with who gets attention or credit for the things *you* are accomplishing through our lives. Our task is to advance *your* irresistible fame and glory, and never our own. For from you, to you, and through you are all things.

 Lord, hear our prayer.
 Amen.[2]

ABOUT THE AUTHOR

SCOTT SAULS SERVES AS SENIOR PASTOR of Christ Presbyterian Church, a multisite church in Nashville, Tennessee (christpres.org). Scott has been married to Patti for twenty-three years and is a dad to Abby and Ellie. Prior to moving to Nashville, Scott was a lead and preaching pastor at New York City's Redeemer Presbyterian Church, planted churches in Kansas City and St. Louis, and taught homiletics (preaching) at Covenant Theological Seminary. Formative experiences have included being an athlete, living in a global city, and suffering through a season of anxiety and depression. A self-described "accidental author," Scott has released three books prior to this one. Influential voices in Scott's life include Tim Keller, C. S. Lewis, Jonathan Edwards, Soong-Chan Rah, Johnny Cash, Joni Eareckson Tada, Paul Tripp, Ann Voskamp, Martin Luther King Jr., Dorothy Sayers, and N. T. Wright. In his free time, you might find Scott relaxing with people or a book, strumming his Gibson guitar, hiking, enjoying live music, or cheering on the St. Louis Cardinals and North Carolina Tar Heels.

Scott blogs weekly at scottsauls.com and has also authored *Jesus Outside the Lines, Befriend,* and *From Weakness to Strength.* You can find him on Twitter and Instagram (@scottsauls) and Facebook (facebook.com/scott.sauls.7).

NOTES

INTRODUCTION

1. Quoted in Philip Yancey, *Soul Survivor* (New York: Random House, 2001), 175. While no original source seems to exist for this quotation, we do know that Gandhi (a) quoted and expressed high regard for Jesus, (b) attributed most of his humanitarian ethic to Jesus, (c) felt grossly mistreated by Christians, whose actions toward him did not reflect Jesus from the New Testament, and (d) very possibly on this basis chose Hinduism over Christianity.

2. Quoted in Fred Metcalf, *The Penguin Dictionary of Modern Humorous Quotations* (London: Penguin Books, 1987), 49.

3. Sarah Pulliam Bailey, "Q & A: Anne Rice on Following Christ Without Christianity," *Christianity Today*, August 17, 2010, http://www.christianitytoday.com/ct/2010/augustweb-only/43-21.0.html.

4. Martyn Lloyd-Jones, *Studies in the Sermon on the Mount* (Grand Rapids: Eerdmans, 1971), 28 (emphasis added).

5. Madeleine L'Engle, *Walking on Water: Reflections on Faith and Art* (New York: Convergent, 2001), 113.

CHAPTER 1: BEING OKAY WITH NOT BEING OKAY

1. Herman Melville, *Moby Dick* (New York: Scribner, 1902), 71.

2. Brennan Manning, *The Ragamuffin Gospel* (Colorado Springs: Multnomah, 2005), 11.

3. William Shakespeare, *Julius Caesar*, act 1, scene 3.

4. Martyn Lloyd-Jones, *Studies in the Sermon on the Mount* (Grand Rapids: Eerdmans, 1971), 34.

5. Samuel Johnson quotes from Tullian Tchividjian, *One Way Love: Inexhaustible Grace for an Exhausted World* (Colorado Springs: David C Cook, 2013), 208–9.

6. *Encyclopedia Britannica*, s.v. "Samuel Johnson," by Robert Folkenfik, accessed July 23, 2018, https://www.britannica.com /biography/Samuel-Johnson.

7. Blaise Pascal, *Pensées* (New York: Penguin Books, 1966), #409.

8. Brennan Manning, *Abba's Child: The Cry of the Heart for Intimate Belonging* (Colorado Springs: NavPress, 2015), 42.

9. See Matthew 26:69–75 and John 20:24–29.

10. I credit my good friend Pastor Scotty Smith for this thought.

CHAPTER 2: GETTING OUR HEADS STRAIGHT

1. C. S. Lewis, *Reflections on the Psalms* (New York: Harvest/Harcourt Books, 1986), 55.

2. Benjamin B. Warfield, "The Testimony of the Holy Spirit to the Bible," *Presbyterian and Reformed Review* 6, no. 23 (July 1895): 78 (emphasis added).

3. Westminster Confession of Faith.

4. Antony Theodore, "Let Your Religion Be a Love Affair," PoemHunter, https://www.poemhunter.com/poem /let-your-religion-be-a-love-affair/.

5. William Cowper, "Love Constraining to Obedience."

6. Quoted in William Dennison, *Essays in the Eschaton* (Eugene, OR: Wipf & Stock, 2015), 40.

7. Francis Schaeffer, *He Is There and He Is Not Silent* (Chicago: Tyndale, 2001).

8. *Encyclopedia Britannica*, s.v. "Jonathan Edwards," by Thomas A. Schafer, accessed July 24, 2018, https://www.britannica.com /biography/Jonathan-Edwards.

9. Jonathan Edwards, *The Works of President Edwards*, (New York: Robert Carter and Brothers, 1881), 1: 21–22.
10. Heidelberg Catechism (1563), question and answer 1.
11. C. S. Lewis, *The Complete C. S. Lewis Signature Classics* (New York: HarperOne, 2002), 503.

CHAPTER 3: SAVORING THE PRECIOUS CHRIST

1. C. S. Lewis, *Mere Christianity* (New York: Harper Collins, 1952), 134.
2. Westminster Shorter Catechism, question 1.
3. Blaise Pascal, *Pensées* (New York: Penguin Books, 1966), 75.
4. *The Lord of the Rings: The Two Towers*, directed by Peter Jackson (Burbank, CA: New Line Cinema, 2002).
5. Robert Robinson, "Come, Thou Fount of Every Blessing" (1757).
6. Daniel Schorn, "Transcript: Tom Brady, Part 3; Tom Brady Talks to Steve Croft," CBS News, November 4, 2005, https://www .cbsnews.com/news/transcript-tom-brady-part-3/.
7. Timothy Keller, *Counterfeit Gods* (New York: Penguin, 2009).
8. Charles Haddon Spurgeon, *The Treasury of David* (Peabody, MA: Hendrickson, 1988), 356.
9. C. S. Lewis, *The Weight of Glory and Other Addresses* (New York: HarperOne, 1980), 26.
10. C. S. Lewis, *Mere Christianity* (New York: HarperOne, 1980), 50.

CHAPTER 4: PRACTICING TRANSPARENCY AND KINDNESS

1. Thomas Wolfe, "The Anatomy of Loneliness," *American Mercury* 53, no. 214 (October 1941).
2. *Zelig*, directed by Woody Allen (Burbank, CA: Warner Bros., 1983).
3. Brennan Manning, *Abba's Child: The Cry of the Heart for Intimate Belonging* (Colorado Springs: NavPress, 2015), 15.
4. This quote is sometimes attributed to Groucho Marx.
5. Quoted in Scotty Smith, *Objects of His Affection* (West Monroe, LA: Howard, 2001), 68.
6. C. S. Lewis, *The Four Loves* (New York: Harcourt Brace, 1988), 121.

7. Quoted in Tony Reinke, "The Purifying Power of Delight in Christ," *Desiring God* (blog), August 7, 2012, http://www.desiringgod.org/articles/the-purifying-power-of-delight-in-christ.

8. Ann Voskamp, Twitter post, June 6, 2014, 4:57 a.m., https://twitter.com/annvoskamp/status/474882708082941953.

CHAPTER 5: PERFORMING SOUL-SURGERY ON ONE ANOTHER

1. This clever quip did not originate with me. I saw it on Twitter recently, cited as being from an anonymous source.

2. Dietrich Bonhoeffer, *Life Together* (New York: Harper & Row, 1954), Kindle edition.

3. John de Grutchy, ed., *Dietrich Bonhoeffer: Witness to Jesus Christ* (Minneapolis: Fortress Press, 1991), 182.

4. Quoted in Larry Alex Taunton, "Listening to Young Atheists: Lessons for a Stronger Christianity," *Atlantic*, June 6, 2013, http://www.theatlantic.com/national/archive/2013/06/listening-to-young-atheists-lessons-for-a-stronger-christianity/276584/2/.

5. Rebecca Manley Pippert, *Hope Has Its Reasons* (Downers Grove, IL: InterVarsity, 2001), 99.

6. Jeff Hays, "I Love Beer and Jesus," *Scott Sauls* (blog), July 3, 2017, https://scottsauls.com/2017/07/i-love-beer-and-jesus/.

7. Anne Lamott, "Anne Lamott Shares All That She Knows: 'Everyone Is Screwed Up, Broken, Clingy, and Scared,'" Salon, April 10, 2015, https://www.salon.com/2015/04/10/anne_lamott_shares_all_that_she_knows_everyone_is_screwed_up_broken_clingy_and_scared/.

8. Joseph Hart, "Come Ye Sinners, Poor and Wretched," (1759).

9. Scott Sauls, "Last Year, Self-Loathing Ruined My Easter, and I'm Sort of Glad That It Did," *Scott Sauls* (blog), April 17, 2017, https://scottsauls.com/2017/04/confessions/.

10. Dan B. Allender and Tremper Longman III, *Intimate Allies: Rediscovering God's Design for Marriage and Becoming Soul Mates for Life* (Wheaton, IL: Tyndale, 1995).

11. Quoted in Vivek Mathur, *Cracking into Super Brains with 6,000 Supreme Quotes* (New Delhi: Studera Press, 2017), 376.
12. You can read more about Jim Morrison's tragic story in Jerry Hopkins and Daniel Sugerman, *No One Here Gets Out Alive: The Biography of Jim Morrison* (New York: Warner, 1980).
13. Although this quote is sometimes attributed to Oscar Wilde, the actual source is unknown.

CHAPTER 6: EMBRACING HOPE INSIDE
THE FAIRY TALE THAT'S TRUE

1. William Shakespeare, *Macbeth*, act 5, scene 5.
2. Quoted in Chris Armstrong, "J. R. R. Tolkien and C. S. Lewis: A Legendary Friendship," *Christianity Today*, August 8, 2008, http://www.christianitytoday.com/history/2008/august/j-r-r-tolkien-and-c-s-lewis-legendary-friendship.html.
3. This story was told to our class by Prof. Jerram Barrs at Covenant Seminary in his Apologetics and Outreach class, spring of 1992. Barrs was speaking anecdotally as founder of English L'Abri, and a protégé of Francis Schaeffer himself.
4. Lee Strobel, *The Case for Christ* (Grand Rapids: Zondervan, 1998), Kindle edition.
5. Justin Taylor, "Why It Matters Theologically and Historically That Women Were the First to Discover the Empty Tomb," The Gospel Coalition, April 15, 2014, https://blogs.thegospelcoalition.org/justintaylor/2014/04/15/why-it-matters-theologically-and-historically-that-women-were-the-first-to-discover-the-empty-tomb/.
6. C. S. Lewis, *God in the Dock: Essays on Theology and Ethics* (Grand Rapids: Eerdmans, 1970), 66.
7. Simon Greenleaf, *An Examination of the Testimony of the Four Evangelists by the Rules Administered in Courts of Justice* (Boston: Charles C. Little and James Brown, 1846), 37.
8. Anne Rice, *Called Out of Darkness: A Spiritual Confession* (Canada: Random House, 2008), 155.

9. For further reading on the "many convincing proofs" for Christianity, I recommend *Reason for God* and *Making Sense of God* by Timothy Keller, *Mere Christianity* by C. S. Lewis, *The Case for Faith* by Lee Strobel, *More Than a Carpenter* by Josh McDowell, and *Orthodoxy* by G. K. Chesterton.

10. See the Heidelberg Catechism, question 1.

11. I got this phrase from an album title by my friend and singer -songwriter Jeremy Casella.

12. Andrew Wilson, "The Strange Encouragement of the Church's Appalling History," *Christianity Today*, March 17, 2017, http ://www.christianitytoday.com/ct/2017/april/strange -encouragement-of-churchs-appalling-history.html.

13. R. F. Christian, ed., *Tolstoy's Letters* (Oxford: Athlone Press, 1978), 2: 362–63.

14. I once heard someone attribute this phrase to Ravi Zacharias, spoken in a talk he gave.

15. This term, "expand our 'us,'" originated with one of Christ Presbyterian Church's members, Dr. Brandi Kellett.

16. This paragraph is taken from the vision statement of Christ Presbyterian Church in Nashville, Tennessee. The full statement can be found at christpres.org.

17. C. S. Lewis, *The Last Battle* (London: Macmillan, 1956), 173.

CHAPTER 7: TREASURING THE POOR

1. Daniel T. Niles, *That They May Have Life* (New York: Harper and Brothers, 1951), 96.

2. Nicholas Kristof, "Evangelicals Without Blowhards," *New York Times*, July 30, 2011, http://www.nytimes.com/2011/07/31 /opinion/sunday/kristof-evangelicals-without-blowhards.html (emphasis added).

3. Petr H., "25 Countries with the Lowest Life Expectancy in the World," List 25, updated May 19, 2016, https://list25 .com/25-countries-with-the-lowest-life-expectancy-in-the-world/.

4. Khushboo Sheth, "Countries with the Highest Infant Mortality Rates," WorldAtlas.com, updated April 25, 2017, https://www

.worldatlas.com/articles/countries-with-the-highest-infant
-mortality-rates.html.

5. "11 Facts About Human Trafficking," DoSomething.org, https
://www.dosomething.org/us/facts/11-facts-about-human-trafficking.

6. "US Abortion Patients," infographic, Guttmacher Institute, https
://www.guttmacher.org/united-states/abortion/demographics.

7. N. T. Wright, *Early Christian Letters for Everyone: James, Peter, John and Judah* (London: Westminster John Knox Press, 2011), 10.

8. Quoted in "Life Is Sacred," Human Coalition, https://www
.humancoalition.org/graphics/life-is-sacred/.

9. Quoted in Robert Frank, "Millionaire Says 'Money Prevents Happiness,'" *Wall Street Journal*, February 9, 2010, https
://blogs.wsj.com/wealth/2010/02/09
/millionaire-says-money-prevents-happiness/.

10. Joseph Hart, "Come Ye Sinners, Poor and Wretched," 1759.

CHAPTER 8: EMBRACING WORK AS MISSION

1. To address this pervasive problem of what we might call the "separation of faith and work," our church founded an organization a few years ago called the Nashville Institute for Faith and Work (NIFW). We started NIFW chiefly as a resource to equip Christians in our city with a vision for how their good work—as well as everyone else's good work, whether Christian or not—is a central part of God's plan to heal, renew, and transform the world. The vision statement reads as follows:

"The Nashville Institute for Faith and Work is dedicated to helping individuals and groups integrate their Christian faith into their day-to-day work in a way that brings about human and organizational flourishing in Nashville and beyond. Considering that the average American will spend over 80,000 hours at work over his or her lifetime, it is important to view the workplace as an opportunity to renew individual hearts, communities, and the world. Some are energized by work while others deplore it; some see it as only a source of income while others see it as a source of self-definition and glorification. . . . Understanding and embracing that all good work—not just ministerial, missionary, medical, or non-profit work—matters to God and is fundamental to joining Him in His redemptive plan for this world."

The purpose of this and similar organizations, such as the Washington Institute (Washington, DC), the Institute for Faith, Work, and Economics (McLean, VA), Made to Flourish (Overland Park, KS), and the Redeemer Center for Faith and Work (New York), is to train, equip, and send people out into the world as a means to love God and neighbor through their particular avenue of work.

2. "What Everyone in the World Wants: A Good Job," Gallup, June 9, 2015, http://news.gallup.com/businessjournal/183527 /everyone-world-wants-good-job.aspx (emphasis added).

3. Steve Crabtree, "Worldwide, 13% of Employees Are Engaged at Work," Gallup, October 8, 2013, http://news.gallup.com /poll/165269/worldwide-employees-engaged-work.aspx.

4. *Office Space* quotes, IMDb, http://www.imdb.com/title/tt0151804 /characters/nm0574540?ref_=ttfc_fc_cl_t16.

5. Jacqui Frank and Julie Bort, "Billionaire Minecraft Founder Markus Persson Proves Money Doesn't Buy Happiness," *Business Insider*, October 6, 2015, http://www.businessinsider.com/man -who-sold-minecraft-to-microsoft-markus-persson-success-2015-10.

6. Gary Rivlin, "In Silicon Valley, Millionaires Who Don't Feel Rich," *New York Times*, August 5, 2007, http://www.nytimes .com/2007/08/05/technology/05rich.html.

7. Andrea Park, "Michelle Williams Shares That She Experienced Depression While She Was in Destiny's Child," *Glamour*, October 19, 2017, https://www.glamour.com/story /michelle-williams-depression-destinys-child.

8. Dorothy Sayers, *Why Work? Discovering Real Purpose, Peace, and Fulfillment at Work: A Christian Perspective* (Charleston: Createspace Independent Publishing, 2014), page unknown.

9. I first heard this thought expressed in a sermon by Tim Keller.

10. Friedrich Nietzsche, *Basic Writings of Nietzsche* (New York: Random House, 2000), 274.

11. As quoted in Victor A. Ginsburgh and David Throsby, eds., *Handbook of the Economics of Art and Culture*, (Oxford: Elsevier, 2014), 2: 102.

12. Quoted in David Brooks, *The Road to Character* (New York: Random House, 2015), 84.

13. "What a NASA Janitor Can Teach Us About Living a Bigger Life," 9News.com, December 24, 2014, http://www.9news.com/life/what-a-nasa-janitor-can-teach-us-about-living-a-bigger-life/249959382.

14. Frederick Buechner, *Wishful Thinking: A Theological ABC* (New York: Harper & Row, 1973), 95.

15. Madeleine L'Engle, *Walking on Water: Reflections on Faith and Art* (New York: Convergent, 2001), 42.

16. Timothy Keller with Katherine Leary Alsdorf, *Every Good Endeavor: Connecting Your Work to God's Work* (New York: Penguin, 2014), 15.

CHAPTER 9: LEAVING IT BETTER

1. H. G. Wells, *A Short History of the World*, as quoted in Timothy Keller, *The Reason for God* (New York: Penguin, 2008), 237.

2. Ibid., 237.

3. Quoted in Laurence J. Peter, *Peter's Quotations: Ideas for Our Time* (New York: Harper Collins, 1977).

4. Dan Colman, "Aldous Huxley, Dying of Cancer, Left This World Tripping on LSD (1963)," Open Culture, October 15, 2011, www.openculture.com/2011/10/aldous_huxleys_lsd_death_trip.html.

5. Paul Kurtz and Edwin H. Wilson, *Humanist Manifesto II*, 1973 (emphasis added).

6. Susan Krauss Whitbourne, "Is Facebook Making You Depressed?" *Psychology Today*, October 14, 2017, https://www.psychologytoday.com/us/blog/fulfillment-any-age/201710/is-facebook-making-you-depressed.

7. Some will contend, perhaps correctly, that the "minimum ten percent" principle—based on Malachi 3:10, Matthew 23:23, and

related texts—applies to all charitable giving as opposed to giving it all to the local church. Yet it is hard to deny, once we read the New Testament, that the local church should be the primary recipient of Christian generosity.

8. Ruth Moon, "Are American Evangelicals Stingy?" *Christianity Today*, January 31, 2011, https://www.christianitytoday.com /ct/2011/february/areevangelicalsstingy.html.

9. Ibid.

10. Timothy Keller, *Generous Justice* (New York: Penguin, 2016), Kindle edition.

11. Isaac Watts, "Joy to the World!" (1719).

12. Quoted in John Piper, "All God's Commands Are Possible with God," *Desiring God*, June 9, 1993, https://www.desiringgod.org /articles/all-gods-commands-are-possible-with-god.

13. James Davison Hunter, *To Change the World* (New York: Oxford University Press, 2010), Kindle edition.

14. Ibid.

A PRAYER FOR IRRESISTIBLE FAITH

1. The phrase "expand our 'us'" originated with our friend and member of our church Dr. Brandi Kellett.

2. Adapted from "Dream for a Better Tomorrow," Christ Presbyterian Church, Nashville, Tennessee (christpres.org).